HUSKYMANIA

VILLARD
NEW YORK

HUSKY MANIA

The Inside Story of the Rise of
UConn's Men's and Women's
Basketball Teams

Jim Shea

Library of Congress Cataloging-in-Publication Data
Shea, Jim.
Huskymania: the inside story of the rise of UConn's men's and women's
basketball teams / Jim Shea.—1st ed.
p.   cm.
ISBN 0-679-44887-X
1. University of Connecticut—Basketball. I. Title.
GV885.43.U44S54   1996
796.323'63'09746—dc20   95-25435

Manufactured in the United States of America
2   4   6   8   9   7   5   3
First Edition

Book design by Tanya M. Pérez

To Jan, Kaitie, and Lisa.
And to Sis.

Acknowledgments

Thanks to Esther Newberg, a loyal fan with juice; to David Rosenthal, Peter Gethers, and Amy Scheibe at Random House; to Tim Tolokan for his time and guidance; to Barb Kowal for her input; to Jim Calhoun, Geno Auriemma, Chris Dailey, Howie Dickenman, and Meghan Pattyson for their candor; to Pat Meiser-McKnett, who saw it all; to Rebecca Lobo, who squeezed me in; to my colleagues at *The Hartford Courant*, from whose work I appropriated much, in particular: Ken Davis, Tom Yantz, Greg Garber, and Bruce Berlet; to the *Courant*'s photo department, especially Karen Lavallee; to Jan, Lisa, and Kaitie Shea, who excused my prolonged neglect; and to the many others who were so willing to help.

Contents

HUSKYMANIA

Huskymania

On the morning of February 14, 1995, the state of Connecticut led the nation in several categories:

Percentage of adults with bachelor's degrees or higher.

Scientists and engineers per 100,000 population.

Helicopter and submarine sales.

Per capita personal income.

Public school teachers' salaries.

Gasoline tax rate.

Oh, and in college basketball.

The previous evening, following a 77-70 weekend victory over Syracuse at the Carrier Dome, the University of Connecticut men's basketball team had been voted number one in the Associated Press poll, receiving fifty of sixty-six first-place ballots. It was the first time a UConn men's basketball team had ever achieved the top ranking. But that was only of secondary historical significance.

In being named number one, the UConn men joined the UConn women's team at the top, marking the first time in NCAA history that the men's and women's teams from the same university held the number one designation at the same time.

The women had grown accustomed to the top spot by this time, having been elevated on January 17, following their nationally televised victory over then number one Tennessee at the Harry A. Gampel Pavilion. In this mid-January poll, the 19-0 women had garnered thirty-two of the thirty-three first-place votes.

Mike Eisenberg, a professor of information studies at Syracuse University, was asked to determine the mathematical probability of the UConn men's and women's simultaneous reign. He calculated that with 302 Division I men's teams and 293 Division I women's teams and all things being equal, the chances of this happening in any one week were 1 in 88,486. Joe Lang, the director of athletics for administration at Georgetown University, took the glass-is-half-empty approach, concluding that there is a 99.91 percent probability that in any one week, the men's and women's teams from the same school would not be ranked number one.

In more down-to-earth terms, a Las Vegas "sports consultant" put the odds as high as 300 to 1. He also said that because polls were involved and voting was a key element, it was a wagering proposition with which he and his associates would never become involved.

"It was lonesome at the top, so we're glad the men joined

us," All-American Rebecca Lobo joked. "We have been hoping for this all season. It's a cliché, but we both have Connecticut on our uniforms and there is nothing better for this state."

And what a state the state was in.

The front pages of morning newspapers screamed number one in type sizes usually reserved for declarations of war or moon walks. Local television stations led their ubiquitous news shows and news updates with the story, managing in the process to claim a certain amount of credit. Radio jocks fielded calls from listeners who often could only articulate their feelings with joyful cries of "Yes" and "Number one, baby."

On the streets, total strangers exchanged high fives. UConn hats, jackets, and shirts seemed to be everywhere. A button-down insurance employee painted his face blue and white, went to work, and *wasn't* called in for a little chat with the boss.

"Unless you're the lead dog," a newspaper vendor repeatedly told customers as he made change, "the view never changes."

At the Sugar Shack doughnut shop near the UConn campus in Storrs, there was a run on "Husky bones," doughnuts shaped like small dog biscuits. Customers entering the popular spot were greeted by a short poem on the door, penned by one of the owners:

Never in history has it been done,
When men and women were No. 1.

The Huskies did it, I'm filled with glee,
So again, today, the coffee is free.

At the UConn Coop, sales of Huskies merchandise were unusually brisk, shoppers picking through the many racks of sweatshirts, shorts, jackets, and hats. On order, and eagerly awaited, were a batch of "No. 1" T-shirts.

The Huskymania this morning even extended into the highest echelons of power in Storrs, Hartford, and Washington, D.C.

UConn president Harry J. Hartley came to work wearing a white sweater with a Husky dog stitched into the front, blue sweatpants, and a red, white, and blue jacket with a Husky dog on the back. Hartley was beaming for two reasons. He is a close friend and frequent running partner of men's head coach Jim Calhoun. And Hartley knew all the publicity the school was receiving, locally and nationally, would be good for the university in terms of enrollment interest and alumni and corporate contributions.

At the state capital in Hartford, newly elected governor John G. Rowland was offering praise and promises: "This gives us the moral boost that we have needed, especially with what has gone on in the state over the past couple of years. . . . So we'll do our part—the state—in terms of taxpayer dollars. . . . We need to make sure that we rebuild that campus and make sure that it is the bright, shining example that we want for the rest of the system."

In Washington, United States senator Christopher J. Dodd was crowing about UConn basketball to one and all and making plans to attend that evening's game between the UConn men and Georgetown. Connecticut's junior senator, Joseph I. Lieberman, a man who has worn a UConn hat into the Senate chambers, was giving a speech when one of his colleagues held up a handwritten sign reading "Go Hoyas," referring to Georgetown.

When this most glorious day finally gave way to night, Connecticut's delirious fans turned on their televisions to catch the game with Georgetown. In the Hartford/New Haven television market, 40 percent of all people watching television that evening, about 240,000 households, would tune in to see the Huskies beat Georgetown for the second time in the season to improve their record to 20-1 and preserve their ranking.

Four days later, however, a sky-high Villanova team would come to Storrs and soundly defeat UConn. And on the following Monday, the men's number one ranking would be lost. The men would go on to post a 23-3 regular-season record and for the second straight year win the Big East regular-season title.

Although they would lose to Villanova again in the Big East Tournament championship game, the men would go on to become a number two seed in the West Regional of the NCAA Tournament. There, they would score impressive victories over Tennessee-Chattanooga, Cincinnati, and Maryland. But they would fall just short against the eventual national champion, UCLA, losing 102-96 in the regional final.

Although the week of February 12–18 was the high point for the UConn men in terms of national attention, the season overall was highly successful, one in which they:

- Finished the year at 28-5, setting a school record of 57-10 over the past two years. Only Arkansas recorded more victories during the period.
- Became the first Big East school to win outright regular-season conference titles back to back, with identical 16-2 records. Also established conference marks for total victories in a two-year period (thirty-two) and consecutive number of games in first place (thirty-six and counting). In addition, the three victories in the 1995 NCAA Tournament gave the program eleven in the past six years, almost double that of any other Big East school.
- Qualified for postseason play for the eighth year in a row (three NIT, five NCAA), earning their second berth in the "Elite Eight" in the past six years. It also marked the fourth time UConn has appeared in the "Sweet Sixteen" in the 1990s, an accomplishment shared by only five other schools: North Carolina, Arkansas, Duke, Indiana, and Kansas.
- Ended the season ranked number six, never having fallen out of the Top 10.
- Sold out every home game and achieved perhaps the highest local television ratings in the country. On the national level, the team would appear on CBS ten times during the season.
- Saw Jim Calhoun's record at UConn reach 190 victories and 96 losses.

Meanwhile, the UConn women cut a swath through the regular season, mowing down teams by an average of thirty-five points per game, finishing 26-0 and number one. They breezed through the Big East Tournament as expected and entered the NCAA Tournament as the number one seed in the East Regional, where their strength and some excellent timing made them heavy favorites.

In accordance with an NCAA policy that mandates early-round tournament games be played on the higher-seeded team's home court, the UConn women's first two games were scheduled for Gampel Pavilion. But the home-court edge didn't end there. Years earlier, the NCAA had selected Gampel as the site for the East Regional semifinals and finals. That meant the women could play four straight games surrounded by their rabid fans if they continued to win. The huge advantage was not squandered. Aside from a close game against Virginia in the regional final, the team easily made it to the Final Four.

Arriving in Minneapolis, the women were greeted by no small amount of disrespect. Despite being number one, despite a 33-0 record, despite having won their games by an average of almost thirty-five points, despite leading the nation in scoring, shooting percentage, rebounding margin, and shooting defense, many of the "experts" felt this would be the end of the line.

"I don't think there is any question Tennessee is the better team right now," Mimi Griffin, a women's basketball analyst for ESPN, was quoted as saying. "I did the UConn-Tennessee game back in January, and this is a different Tennessee team. I don't care about the rankings. Tennessee really has its form. They are all on the same page now. Tennessee is playing the best it can play."

Stanford, whom UConn would play in the semifinals, was

also expected to present big problems. The Cardinals featured twelve former high school All-Americans and regularly played them all as a means of wearing down the opposition. UConn, for the most part, featured a seven-player rotation. But Stanford proved to be a paper threat. UConn led 44-20 at the half and won by twenty-seven, the largest margin of victory in the fourteen-year history of the Final Four. Now all that stood between UConn and the school's first basketball national championship, between UConn and a perfect season, between UConn and a measure of immortality, was Tennessee.

"I'm not sure anyone can beat Tennessee twice in the same season," UConn head coach Geno Auriemma said at the postgame press conference.

"I don't think Geno believes that," Tennessee head coach Pat Summitt responded. "But I hope he's right."

As the late afternoon game time approached, there was a noticeable lull in the normally brisk Sunday afternoon traffic and a marked decline of shoppers in the stores in and about Connecticut. Everyone, it seemed, was parked in front of a television somewhere.

Local television ratings would later bear this out. Between 3:45 and 6 P.M., two of every three sets in use in Connecticut were tuned to UConn-Tennessee. The game would end up being watched by more people than had ever watched a college basketball game in Connecticut, men's or women's. The viewership in the state surpassed even that for the 1995 Super Bowl.

The game itself matched the hype. Questionable officiating forced UConn to sit down its three All-Americans, Rebecca Lobo, Kara Wolters, and Jen Rizzotti, for much of the first half because of foul trouble. But Tennessee could not exploit the advantage, struggling to build a six-point lead at the break.

Tennessee extended the lead to nine points early in the second half. But UConn continued to play hard, displaying the grit and determination that is the signature of all championship teams. With Lobo leading the way in the final minutes, UConn rallied to win, 70-64, joining the University of Texas (1986) as the only women's team to go through an entire season undefeated.

The joy on the floor of the Target Center in Minneapolis was equaled by the euphoria, the pride, and, yes, the relief that swept over Connecticut. Drivers honked their horns and flashed their headlights. Bar patrons spilled out onto the streets in celebration; at the student union in Storrs, a crowd of about 150 high-fived and hugged. Connecticut, tiny Connecticut, was the home of the national champions.

The state's media, which had covered the final game in force, seemed surprised, ill prepared for the outcome. WFSB, the local CBS affiliate on which the game had been viewed, received angry calls when the network left the scene rather than staying for the postgame ceremonies and celebration. Radio station WTIC, which had broadcast the game, cut to a canned business program after a standard-length postgame show. All the local news telecasts led with the game but were able to provide only minimal coverage beyond basic stories. People wanted to express their feelings, share their unbridled happiness, and were frustrated by the absence of media vehicles. So on Sunday, UConn fans basically savored the triumph in private, postponing the public outpouring until the next day.

Auriemma was just concluding a congratulatory telephone conversation with President Clinton when the phone at *The Hartford Courant*, Connecticut's largest newspaper, began to ring. During the course of the evening, hundreds of people would call, all with the same question. When would the women's plane be landing at Bradley International Airport?

The following morning, the *Courant* wrapped the paper in a ten-page special section on the game. The main headline consisted of a single word: PERFECT! The lead picture showed a smiling Auriemma being carried off the court by his players. All day long, people read about the team, called radio shows, exchanged knowing winks and hugs, and waited for the women, *their* women, to come home.

At the state capital, Rowland again talked about the boost the team had given the recession-ravaged state. In Washington, Congresswoman Rosa De Lauro held up a Husky T-shirt to applause from other House members. Senators Lieberman and Dodd spoke of the team on the Senate floor. Even Bill Bradley from New Jersey, a former player for the New York Knicks, rose to praise the team.

When the UConn women's plane finally landed at about 6 P.M., some 1,500 fans were there to greet them. Many had waited in a biting wind for more than two hours to cheer and stick their fingers through a chain-link fence in hopes they might be grazed by one of the players.

Local television news teams were also there in force. They would make up for Sunday's undercoverage with overkill, if such a thing were possible with this story given the public's appetite. The stations began covering the team's arrival prior to 5 P.M., and some would stay with the story until 9 P.M., skipping their local and national news shows in the process. They would all be rewarded for their efforts with another round of huge ratings.

Rebecca Lobo was the first player off the plane. Waiting for her at the bottom of the stairs was Governor Rowland, who shook each player's hand and presented each with a bouquet of roses. After the women had greeted waiting family and friends, interacted with the crowd, and talked to the media, they boarded a bus for the trip back to Storrs, where fans were assembling to greet them at packed Gampel Pavilion.

Along the road to Storrs an impromptu parade formed. Hundreds of cars pulled to the side of the highway to wave as the team bus went past. At overpasses, fans hung congratulatory banners. Even the state Department of Transportation got into the spirit, using computerized highway warning signs to flash "UConn Women's Basketball" and "National Champions 1995."

As the women, jaws ajar, pressed their faces against the windows taking in the scene, not believing what they were seeing, Auriemma, seated next to his wife, Kathy, was quiet, pensive. "I think I was suffering from what women suffer right after they give birth, postpartum depression," Auriemma says. "It hit me right away. I was just so tired. All the stuff that we had held in, all this focus, all this idea of every day, be good today, be good today, never giving yourself a chance to look ahead or look behind . . . I just didn't have anything left. I just didn't have any energy left. And when I was on the bus and watching what the reaction was, I was thinking, man, I just don't know if I can do it one more day."

At Gampel Pavilion, the eight-thousand-plus gave the team and coaches a thunderous ovation as they entered the arena and mounted a makeshift stage. Swaying back and forth, the fans chanted "We're number one" and sang "We Are the Champions." The moment was emotional, electric. And television brought it into homes all over Connecticut.

The following night, television sets would also glow late, as fans stayed up to watch Lobo on "Late Night with David Letterman." It didn't stop there. Lobo and her teammates would also be the guests on many other national talk shows in the following days, including "Regis and Kathie Lee."

Everyone, it seemed, wanted a piece of the champions. The UConn sports information office was swamped with requests. The White House called and issued an invitation for the entire team to appear. The mayor of Hartford announced he would throw a parade, and a month later 100,000 people lined city streets on a Saturday afternoon to hail their heroines one more time.

Even *Sports Illustrated* couldn't resist. For only the third time in the magazine's history, a separate cover was issued for the Northeast region, featuring an action photo of Jen Rizzotti. The original 66,000 issues were gone as soon as they hit the stands. *Sports Illustrated* then printed an additional 111,000 copies for distribution, and they too were snapped up.

Even while the hot, alluring flame of new celebrity burned, there was already talk of next season. In 1995–96, the UConn men and women would be expected to vie again for the national championship. Both basketball programs were now among the very top in the nation. Success at the highest level was now the standard, not just some one-shot caress of fate. And yet it was just a decade ago that UConn basketball dwelled in the Big East cellar and such lofty goals were beyond comprehension.

Associate women's head coach Chris Dailey often reflected on how far the team had come in ten years, as crowds greeted planes and fans lined highways, as the media swarmed and politicians elbowed for spots on the bandwagon, as President Clinton called, as eight thousand voices sang "We Are the Champions," and as 100,000 parade goers jammed the streets of Hartford.

"It was very emotional on the bus ride to Storrs from the airport," Dailey says, "and I'm not an emotional person. Geno had come over and was standing in the aisle and we were looking at all the people lining the highway and I was just thinking how far we had come. And just what a special place this is because I don't know that this happens everywhere or could happen anywhere else but Connecticut."

The Arrival of Geno Auriemma

The task of finding a new women's basketball coach was not going well in the late spring of 1985. Several candidates had been interviewed for the vacant position, and none had seemed to possess the proper mix of personality, vision, and coaching ability the committee was seeking. The final candidate was a smooth-talking, suave-looking, thirty-one-year-old assistant coach from the University of Virginia named Geno Auriemma.

"We could hardly wait until he got here," recalls committee chairperson Pat Meiser-McKnett, the associate director of athletics at the time. "Everyone had told us that we were really going to like this guy, and at the point that he was interviewed, we were pretty discouraged."

In the weeks before Auriemma's interview, each committee member had been contacted by someone in the collegiate-athletic community on behalf of the applicant. Meiser-McKnett's call had come from Debbie Ryan, the head women's basketball coach at Virginia. "Debbie said to me, 'Pat, he's the reason we got it done here,' and for her to say that to me, personally, well, that was a huge concession."

As significant as Ryan's confession might have been, Meiser-McKnett still had a personal agenda. "I was committed to hiring the best woman for the position," she says. "If there were two candidates who graded out the same and one was male and the other female, we were clearly going to take the female."

After talking with the players, however, Meiser-McKnett backed off some from her initial stance: "I had made the assumption that the players wanted a woman. But I found they really didn't care. Most of them had been coached by men in high school, and it wasn't as much an issue for them as it was for me at the time."

Meiser-McKnett had come to UConn after twelve years as the women's basketball coach at Penn State. With her she brought a soft spot for women's basketball and a conviction that a successful program could capture the fancy of Connecticut's ardent basketball fans. It was not a widely shared vision, a reality underscored by the fact that the new coach would not be hired until August, a mere two months before the start of the season.

Relative to men's basketball at UConn, the women's program was still in its infancy in 1985–86. Prior to 1974, women's basketball had been little more than an intramural program, although there was some intercollegiate competition. In 1974, women's basketball was removed from the realm of the university's physical education department and brought under the aegis of the department of athletics. The 1974–75 season is considered the beginning of the "modern era" of women's basketball at UConn. It is also the point from which records were kept.

To say the women's basketball program had fostered a tradition of mediocrity would be understatement. In its first eleven years, the program had posted only one winning season, and that was 16-14 (1980–81). Following that modest success, subsequent teams were 36-74 over the next four seasons and in the Big East had won a total of four games in three seasons. In truth, the program did not need a coach as much as it needed a messiah.

Search committee member Tim Tolokan, associate athletic director for communications, saw Auriemma as a source of salvation: "We were looking for someone who was not going to allow the status quo to be okay, and we saw that in Geno. He was such an aggressive assistant at Virginia that I think the head coach there was intimidated by his presence. I, and I think others on the search committee, took that as a positive. He wanted excellence. He wanted to succeed. He was going to work within the system, but also be hard-charging."

While the search committee was checking out Auriemma, he was doing the same to the University of Connecticut. He didn't like much of what he saw, but he did like the situation. "After I met the people on the committee, I wanted the opportunity to say yes to the job," Auriemma says. "I didn't know if I would take it, but I wanted them to offer it to me. I told the committee how I would do things. I explained how I did things at Virginia and how I would do it here. And I told them I would do things in a way that would make them proud."

The search committee got the message. "Geno left us with the clear impression that he could get it done," Meiser-McKnett says.

As part of his interview visit, Auriemma was taken to the Big East baseball tournament going on at Muzzy Field in Bristol and introduced around. "I remember watching him interact with people," Barb Kowal, associate director of athletic communications, says. "He was very charming, confident, had a sense of humor, and just seemed very at ease with people. I remember thinking, wow, that could take you far in the recruiting world."

Although Auriemma was successfully selling himself, he was far from sold on the situation he would be walking into. Long-range, he was viewing the job as a stepping-stone, a place to build a reputation before moving on. "I saw the negatives," Auriemma says. "I thought I would try and overcome them for as long as I could and at some point, if I saw that I couldn't, then I was going to leave. I wasn't going to kill myself if there weren't going to be changes. I would go someplace else to win a national championship."

Auriemma was hired with a minimum of fanfare. "We didn't even have a press conference," Kowal says, "because quite frankly there was not a lot of interest. We sent out press releases, and most papers ran these little three-inch stories or mentioned it in the news of the day. That's where the program was at the time."

Athletic director John Toner generously gave Auriemma a five-year contract. Obviously, building a successful women's basketball program was going to take a while. It was also going to take help, which is the first thing Auriemma went looking for.

"I remember Pat Meiser asked me who I would hire as an assistant if I got the job, and I told her Chris Dailey," Auriemma says. "It was the first lie I told here. And Pat said, 'What makes you think you can get her? She's the top assistant at Rutgers, she played there, why would she want to come here?' And I said, 'Why would any kid want to come here?' I thought this would be a good test of my theory that recruiting was about people, not facilities."

Auriemma's pitch to Dailey was that at UConn she would have an opportunity to build a program from the ground up. "What did you do to build the program at Rutgers?" he asked her. "You helped them win a national championship as a player, here you have a chance to do that as a coach."

Dailey, then twenty-six, bought in, becoming Auriemma's first and still most valuable recruit. "I thought it was important for me to learn what it takes to build a program," says Dailey, who is now associate head coach. "At Rutgers, I was just maintaining. I knew that if I was ever going to get a head coaching job, it would be at a school like Connecticut. I wasn't going to be offered the job at Tennessee or Louisiana Tech."

In her visit to the campus, Dailey didn't bother to look around much. Good thing, because even a cursory tour might have dissuaded her. In terms of facilities, UConn was a beat-up, oil-burning clunker trying to run with the sleek, shiny, luxury models that made up the rest of the Big East Conference.

The women's basketball office was walk-in-closet size, consisting of a desk each for Auriemma and Dailey and a couch and coffee table for the two part-time assistants. A lone secretary was shared with seventeen other sports, which meant that it was often necessary to type one's own letters, stuff one's own envelopes.

"I had a black rotary phone that took forever to dial," Auriemma says. "But then Dom Perno, a men's basketball coach in the Big East Conference, had the same thing."

Dailey's phone situation was even worse. "I had to share my phone line with the men's track coach," she says. "I couldn't even answer the phone and say 'women's basketball.' And if the track coach got a call, I would have to run down the hall and see if he was in."

Going on the road to recruit afforded little escape from the Mickey Mouse operation. Transportation came by means of the university motor pool, and until Auriemma and Dailey arranged a lease with a local dealership, they often arrived at a prospect's home in a wheezing 1982 Chevy Chevette complete with the State of Connecticut logo on the door.

If the office accommodations were second-rate, the conditions at the Field House were of fleabag quality. The roof leaked, the locker rooms were shabby, and the walls needed painting. For the women's practices, a large curtain would be drawn around a portion of the court. And while that may have created a modicum of privacy, it did nothing to block the noise. On any given day, track, baseball, and intramural athletes would be using the building at the same time.

Kowal has lingering recollections of a starter's pistol going off again and again as sprinters were put through their paces.

For Auriemma, it was the crack of the bat: "Guys would be hitting baseballs in the cage. They were not even guys on the team, just some kids off the street who wanted to get some swings in."

The Field House was also the venue for games, which were intimate little affairs featuring the two teams, some officials, and, on a good afternoon, perhaps fifty fans. "The games weren't a big premium on my time," Kowal says. "I would run back and forth between them and maybe a gymnastics meet.

"We would set up one table at courtside, and volunteers would run the clock and keep score. I might put out a hundred and twenty-five rosters for the fans and pick about half of them up at the end of the evening. Sporadically, we might get a writer to a game, and if a photographer from one of the newspapers came, that was a big coup. There was no media interest, and it was a struggle to just get the score in the agate the next day. We couldn't even get papers to run the standings until 1990. Compare that to the Tennessee game on January sixteenth, when we had a hundred and fifty-six members of the media at courtside.

"If a writer did show up in those days, Geno would spend twenty-five minutes after the game talking to him or her. And more often than not, the reporter would walk away thinking something might be going on here. I still have this mental picture of Geno standing in this dark little hallway holding court. He's a great dreamer, the best idea man you will ever find, and, after a while, he began to capture people."

To drum up interest, Auriemma and Dailey held clinics for high school coaches, invited high school and junior high school teams to games, *anything* to get some people in the stands. In fact, UConn women's basketball was a good value —there was no charge for tickets. Another early ploy was "Girl Scout Day," when area troops would be invited to come and participate in such activities as banner contests.

"Looking back, I wonder how we managed to do what we did," Dailey says. "But at the time, we didn't think about it. If you are competitive, if you are a survivor, then you do what you have to do to get it done. We never worried about what we didn't have. We only talked about what we had, and at the time all we had was us. We had to sell us and what it was going to be. I guess we also knew that people had a lot of respect for Geno and me as recruiters, so we figured if we weren't successful, people would blame it on UConn."

Amid trying to establish contact with the high school basketball coaches all over Connecticut. Amid an intense recruiting expansion in which the range was extended to include the territory covered by the Big East Conference. Amid a thousand little battles over lockers and practice time and a sign over the locker-room door and color photos in the media guide and uniforms and even sneakers, they played the 1985–86 season. And when it was over, the UConn women had compiled a 12-15 record, which featured a record four Big East victories, including successive wins over Georgetown, Syracuse, and Seton Hall.

"I don't think I've ever had a team work harder than that first team," Auriemma says. "That's still my favorite team of all time to coach. They were lousy, but they didn't know it. What I learned from that year is that if you give kids some hope they will respond. I don't think I have ever had a team respond better to what I tried to do than that team. We were twelve and fifteen, and everyone was ecstatic. We got out of the eight-nine game in the Big East Tournament, and Peggy Walsh made first team Big East. Peggy Walsh will remember me for as long as she lives because in her senior year she had her greatest season.

"That season also taught me that it's not about winning because two years later we were seventeen and eleven, and I hated every kid on the team and they hated me. We were squeezing wins out, but they hated it. So, seventeen wins, horrible, twelve wins, I tell you I never slept better or enjoyed myself more than that year."

In an office near Auriemma's, however, men's basketball coach Dom Perno was finding the going increasingly tough. While Auriemma was busy battling the bureaucracy and trying to build for the future, Perno was fighting a full-fledged war and trying simply to survive the present.

Perno had been under intense pressure going into the 1985–86 season, his ninth, though he denied feeling it. During the past three seasons, his teams had been 12-16, 13-15, and 13-15. Another losing season and Perno would have the worst four-year record in the modern era of UConn men's basketball.

Although UConn had not won much during the period, season-ticket sales (8,000), overall attendance (224,434 in 1984–85), and media coverage (seventeen dailies) had not dwindled. That was the good news—and the bad news. Fans of Connecticut basketball have always been intimately in-volved with the team. When things are going well, they can provide a positive presence. But when the team is losing, they can be most unpleasant.

Perno had become the focal point of the fans' wrath the previous season. As the losses mounted, the nasty letters, the heckling, the booing, the berating on radio talk shows had grown steadily more abusive. As far as the fans were concerned, this was Perno's last chance. If he didn't produce a winner, he could either fall on his sword or be axed.

Wrote UConn beat writer Ken Davis of *The Hartford Courant* prior to the first game: "This season may be more pressure packed than any other. Whether he wants to admit it, another losing season would be a big blow to the UConn program, not to mention Perno's future at the school."

Perno had been a popular figure around the Storrs campus since his playing days. He was cocaptain of the 1963–64 team that advanced to the NCAA Regional Finals. In the regional semifinals, Perno had gained a place in Connecticut basketball lore when in the waning seconds he had stolen the ball from Princeton All-American Bill Bradley to seal the victory.

After coaching at the high school level for several years, Perno became an assistant coach under Dee Rowe at UConn, a position he held for five years. In 1977, he became head coach when Rowe stepped down. In UConn's first three years in the newly formed Big East Conference, Perno posted records of 20-9, 20-9, and 17-11, qualifying for the National Invitation Tournament each year. But then came the three straight losing seasons, the combined record of 38-46, the lack of postseason participation, and, now, the widespread disenchantment.

Perno felt he had the makings of a good team. He thought

he had depth and a nice mix of new and experienced players. Back was his senior point guard and leading scorer, Earl Kelley. There was also a promising freshman from Buffalo on the team named Cliff Robinson, a player who would go on to become a major NBA star with the Portland Trail Blazers.

A potentially devastating problem involving Kelley had been cleared up in October. He had been involved in an incident that centered around the alleged abduction of another student. There were serious questions as to whether he would be able to play. A disciplinary committee eventually voted to punish Kelley but also to let him participate.

The way Perno saw the Big East shaping up was with Syracuse clearly at the top and everyone else kind of grouped together. The Big East coaches saw it a little differently, picking UConn to finish eighth, a step below where they had ended up the previous year. However you sliced it, the season ahead was going to be challenging. *Basketball Times* magazine determined UConn to have the seventh-toughest schedule in the nation, among 232 Division I schools.

Although fifteen of the twenty-eight teams that UConn was scheduled to meet would ultimately play in the postseason, things started off well. UConn won its first eight games, including an impressive victory over Minnesota. Although none of the victories were against top-notch competition, they were nonetheless good enough to keep the circling critics at bay.

In a game that would become noteworthy for its historical irony, UConn suffered its first defeat in the championship game of the Connecticut Mutual Classic. The opponent was Northeastern University. The coach, Jim Calhoun.

From this point on, things began to go rapidly downhill as

UConn lost five of its next seven games. In early January, Terry Coffey, a sophomore reserve guard, was forced to leave the team because of academic problems. He joined Al Armstrong, a walk-on, who had become ineligible earlier in the season. Things were beginning to turn ugly. Following a loss to Villanova at the Hartford Civic Center on January 13, the crowd of 12,129 showered the court with coins as a mark of their frustration.

By early February, Dr. John T. Casteen, who had become the eleventh president of the University of Connecticut the previous July, had seen enough. He announced the formation of a blue-ribbon commission called the President's Task Force on Athletics.

Casteen asked for a report by May on how the university could:

- Improve academic performance among athletes.
- Build more support for athletic programs while using athletes to foster the university's image and increase public awareness of academic, research, and public-service programs.
- Make sure that athletic funding was done in such a manner that it contributed, rather than detracted, from the university's integrity.

Casteen was particularly distressed by a study of graduation rates that had been done the previous year. The study showed that six years after they had entered school in 1979, the overall graduation rate for that freshman class was 66 percent. But for football players the rate was 51 percent, for basketball players just 25 percent. And that dismal rate was about to get even worse.

On February 14, 1986, exactly nine years prior to the very day that the UConn men and women would be hailed throughout the United States for having achieved the pinnacle of college basketball achievement, Earl Kelley would become the third UConn player to be declared academically ineligible for failing to make up work from the previous semester. Outrage and dismay reverberated throughout the state. How could this have been allowed to happen? In retrospect, this Valentine's Day would be the low point in the modern history of UConn basketball.

With Kelley and his 19.6 points and 6.4 assists per game gone, Perno had to go back to training camp in midseason and start from scratch. He had lost his point guard, his offense, his team. And his constituency had lost its patience.

John Woodcock, a state representative from South Windsor, let it be known he was considering filing a resolution in the General Assembly aimed at exploring UConn's membership in the Big East. "There is a tremendous reservoir of discontent and frustration," said Woodcock, a season-ticket holder. "You go to games and listen to the fans, and there's a lot of frustration, a lot of anger."

Athletic director John Toner came to Perno's defense, saying his coach's job was not in jeopardy. "I don't feel any differently about Dom than I did a year ago," Toner told the media. "I think he has done a remarkable job under adverse conditions."

Asked if that meant Perno would be back the next season,

Toner said: "I don't think I even have to answer that. I've always stood with Dom."

The season ended with UConn losing its last eight games, including the first game of the Big East Tournament—the sixth straight year they'd been ousted in the first round. The howling for Perno's head grew even more strident. Toner and Perno, who had sixteen months remaining on his contract, had several meetings.

"Dom was under pressure to resign," says Pat Meiser-McKnett, then associate athletic director. "Whether the university supported him or not, he was taking a beating."

"Dom went to school at Connecticut," Auriemma says. "He played here, was an assistant and head coach here. He grew up with the people who were here at the time. What was he going to do, bust their balls? That would have been a hard thing for him to do. And I'm not sure rattling their cages would not have just fallen on deaf ears anyhow.

"I watched every day how people treated Dom, and I'll tell you what, I keep that filed away in the back of my mind. There were people who were his friends and buddies when he was in the NCAA Tournament who weren't around at the end. But you know, with everything that was happening to him, he was genuinely happy that things were going better for us. He'd put his arm around me and say, 'This is a great place, the people here are really great. They will do anything for you.' "

On April 11, Perno was still denying rumors that his resignation was imminent. "Right now, I'm the coach. Next year, I'm the coach. After next year, then who the hell knows. . . .

But right now I'm the basketball coach, and I have no other things going. That's it."

Three days later, Perno, forty-four, met with his team for about twenty minutes in the morning. Then, at an emotional press conference, he resigned.

"The end result was that I made the decision for two reasons," Perno said. "My family and the Connecticut family which was my basketball family. . . . I think the decision will be very good for my family, and I think it will provide some daylight for my basketball program."

With that, Dom Perno, who had played for UConn in the old Yankee Conference, served as an assistant coach in the Eastern Collegiate Athletic Conference, and shepherded the school into the Big East, left. The buyout on his contract totaled $87,742. His nine-year record of 139-114 ranked him as the second-winningest coach in UConn history.

"Nothing is going to be different, no matter who they bring in," said newly elected team captain Gerry Besselink dejectedly.

But Besselink was wrong. With Perno's departure, the long, slow, complicated climb to basketball respectability began. Even as Perno had been pondering whether to leave, the roots of resurgence were already being established by the Task Force on Athletics.

"The view of our situation here by many people is that we have had all the tools we needed," Perno had said. "I believe that President Casteen's new committee will prove that has not been the case."

"Did Dom have the tools? Absolutely not," says Meiser-McKnett. "We just weren't, even as a department, focused.

We weren't committed. . . . You have to be a son of a bitch to move things. If you are not willing to do that yourself, you better have someone at your side who is willing to. Quite honestly, in '86, nobody was doing that for Dom, and there were so many things that needed to be done. It was a transitional time."

The task force report ordered by President Casteen would be released less than a month later. And in instance after instance it would document the extent to which Perno's claim rang true. Connecticut basketball was in a sorry state.

The Task Force Report

When Casteen announced the creation of the President's Task Force on Athletics, many assumed he had stacked the committee with people who were disenchanted with the current athletic administration and favored wholesale change. In fact, selection of committee members was largely left to John Toner, an ironic twist since, ultimately, he would be roundly criticized by the very people he selected.

Among the task force members were board of trustees member Gerald J. Lawrence, who served as chairman; vice chairman Corine Nogaard, a professor of accounting; former Republican candidate for governor Lewis B. Rome; Chief Court Administrator Aaron Ment; Pat Meiser-McKnett, associate director of athletics; John L. Allen, a professor of geography; Thomas Poppelwell, associate comptroller; H. Fred

Simons, assistant vice president–Minority Affairs; and Ann Huckenbeck, assistant dean of the School of Business.

As the task force report was nearing completion in May, word about its findings and recommendations began to leak out. But when it was made public at a University Senate meeting on May 12, 1986, few were prepared for its blunt assessments and sweeping recommendations.

"The Division of Athletics has functioned as a virtual island of isolation in the university," the report stated. "It has been autonomous insofar as policy and goal establishment, and has had a reporting relationship to the President that has been more nominal than real."

The task force report also concluded that the theory that athletics and academics were mutually reinforcing had found little acceptance at UConn: "Indeed, if there is one common finding that has resulted from our investigation, it is that the major problem of athletic programs at the university seems to be a problem of attitude, a belief that athletics are not an integral part of the university community, that they are a hindrance to be tolerated but not accommodated, that they are a 'necessary evil' which is unimportant to the overall functioning and well-being of the institution."

Although it did not refer to him by name, the report was also highly critical, harsh even, in its evaluation of Toner's administration: "At the University of Connecticut, the isolation of the division of athletics from the general university community and, in addition, the failure of the division and its director to manage its resources in a wise and effective manner, is largely responsible for the malaise which is so apparent from any close investigation of athletics at this university."

Lawrence said the comments regarding Toner's performance could not be left out. "One person on the committee kept saying, 'Who's in charge? Who's in charge?' After a while we came to realize that somebody is responsible somewhere for something. . . . If we weren't objective and honest, if we didn't say things that are obvious, then everyone would have thought this was a whitewash."

Another task force member, who requested anonymity, was quoted in the newspaper as saying: "You get a feeling when you interview the coaches that there was not much in the way of staff meetings, there wasn't a good forum for the coaches. He [Toner] didn't communicate well with the staff as a whole as far as we could see. He didn't communicate at all with the faculty senate. He couldn't communicate problems to either the housing or food services, or the sports medicine people, so that someone could solve these things."

The report also pointed out that the athletic department could not explain why some sports, such as men's soccer and women's field hockey, were successful, while men's basketball and football were not. Task force members also wondered why the football team had not been consistently successful in twenty years despite having received as many as seventy scholarship students. As for the department's $4.5 million budget that covered twenty-two sports, the report charged that it was handled as one big mass of funds and didn't even include line-item budgets.

The sixty-six-page report made recommendations in four general areas: program development, public relations and finance, academics and athletics, student life and special needs. In the area of program development, the committee recommended that the president and board of trustees define its goals for athletics and demonstrate a commitment to athletic excellence.

Regarding athletics and academics, the report found the current counseling program inadequate and said a new system needed to be implemented with the goal of achieving graduation rates that mirrored at least those of the university as a whole. The report did not favor special courses for athletes but did suggest the institution of a mandatory orientation program for incoming athletes.

Addressing the matter of student life and the special needs of athletes, the report called for separate housing for athletes within existing facilities, later dining hours, and financial aid for summer school and for pursuing a degree after their eligibility expired. In addition, the report called for improvement in the sports medicine department and intramural sports and support for minority students.

As for public relations and finance, the report called for sweeping changes in the way the university presented itself and its athletes, in fund-raising, and in financial planning.

Finally, the report called for Toner to undergo a job evaluation, noting he had not had one in seventeen years.

"The task force report, like all reports of that type, was a tremendously powerful political tool," says Meiser-McKnett, who is now the athletic director at the University of Hartford. "The biggest missing piece at the University of Connecticut was the university embracing athletics. By exposing the books, and they really did, by getting the Lew Romes, the Ann

Huckenbecks, the Gerry Lawrences, the John Allens, the Corine Nogaards to investigate and to buy into the study, the university really did expose itself. And that is what Casteen wanted. He needed support for change, and you get that support when you have a mass of people come in from the outside and evaluate and say, oh, this is bad. We need changes here, this is embarrassing."

Toner's tenure as athletic director was probably numbered the day Casteen arrived in Storrs. The new president had been hired in part because it was believed he could bring UConn into the modern era of college athletics. He had come to UConn from the University of Virginia, a school that had successfully been able to integrate academics and athletics. In 1975, Casteen had been the school's dean of admissions and was instrumental in the successful matriculation of seven-foot, four-inch Ralph Sampson. Casteen was representative of the new era in college athletics, in which the role of athletic director called for strong marketing and administration skills. John Toner was an old-school football guy.

Toner came to UConn in 1966 as the school's twenty-first head football coach. He was hired by the late Homer Babbidge, who served as president from 1962 to 1972. A Yale grad, Babbidge wanted to bring an Ivy League approach to athletics. Philosophically, Babbidge did not want athletics very far removed from the realm of extracurricular activities. In Toner, who had spent nine years as an assistant coach at Columbia, Babbidge felt he had a kindred spirit.

One of Babbidge's directives in regard to downplaying varsity sports was to order the athletic department to offer more scholarships based on financial need rather than athletic prowess. This approach not only prevented coaches from recruiting quality athletes, it also cost the university some outstanding coaching talent. Among the coaches who left UConn during the Babbidge years were Rick Forzano, who went on to coach the Detroit Lions, Sam Rutigliano, who was head coach of the Cleveland Browns, and Lou Holtz, the present football coach at the University of Notre Dame.

Another person lost was head basketball coach Fred Shabel, whom Babbidge passed over for the position of athletic director in 1967, despite the overwhelming endorsement of a search committee. Babbidge feared Shabel would tip the balance too far in favor of athletics.

After Jim Hickey, whom Babbidge hired rather than Shabel, left following two uninspired years, Toner was made athletic director. He assumed the position, in addition to remaining head football coach, in 1969, continuing a fifty-year tradition at UConn of the athletic director coming from the football ranks. In 1971, Toner gave up coaching football to concentrate on the athletic director's job full-time.

In Toner, Babbidge got a man who shared his idealism and made do with what he had. Toner was nothing if not an accommodating team player. When Babbidge asked Toner to transfer $100,000 from his shoestring budget to the library fund, Toner did so. When Glen Ferguson was president and experienced a shortfall of $200,000, Toner gave it to him out of the athletic department budget.

Faced with a myriad of problems at home, many of which he could do nothing about, Toner found refuge on the national scene, where, simultaneously with his UConn A.D. job, he held offices at the highest level in the NCAA for eight years, including the presidency between 1983 and 1985. It was in this capacity that Toner probably made his greatest contributions to intercollegiate athletics. Often problems at his home school were the impetus for his involvement. Toner was instrumental in the implementation of Title IX, which required equal treatment for women's athletics. He also was involved in dividing football into Division 1-A and 1-AA and the passage of the freshman eligibility rules known as Proposition 48.

But these accomplishments came with a price, and that was time away from his primary job in Storrs. Staff members said Toner was absent roughly one third of the time. "Absentee management is acceptable as long as you're leaving the house in good hands when you're gone," John Allen said. "I fault John for that." Present UConn president Harry Hartley, who was vice president of finance and administration at the time and a regular racquetball partner of Toner's, summed it up this way: "John had no management skills. It was that simple."

Perhaps the most striking example of the lack of sophistication with which the division of athletics functioned under Toner was the seat-of-the-pants manner in which UConn decided to join the Big East Conference. Toner was approached about joining the Big East in May of 1979 but was not overly enthusiastic because he didn't particularly like the idea of a basketball-only conference. He also felt a certain amount of loyalty to longtime rivals such as the University of Massachusetts and the University of Rhode Island, who hadn't been invited to join because they had much less appealing television markets.

Toner briefly discussed the new conference with President John A. DiBiaggio, who generally left decisions involving the athletic department to Toner. On May 26, Toner received a phone call informing him that a decision to join the new conference had to be made within twenty-four hours because of pressing considerations, including the start of the fiscal year, scheduling, and a future NCAA berth. The next day, Toner got another call, the essence of which was: In or out? Toner tried to contact DiBiaggio but couldn't. So he made the call himself—in.

"We knew we were in a new arena with Syracuse and St. John's," Toner said, "but I thought if we were ever going to get better, that was the kind of challenge that would stimulate it."

At the NCAA convention in San Diego in January 1987, Casteen broached the subject of Toner's departure. Toner said he needed some time, until February 1. Casteen came home and announced at a trustees meeting that same week that Toner would be stepping down.

Toner was left with no options. On January 21, he resigned. In a terse statement he said he would take a leave of absence for six months and then devote his time to the completion of the new sports center.

Four months later, on May 28, Toner was replaced by William T. "Todd" Turner, the thirty-six-year-old associate director of athletics for sports services at the University of Virginia. Turner, a man with a strong marketing background, would be the first athletic director at UConn in sixty-eight years to not come from a football background.

"John Toner overstayed his era," said Corine Nogaard.

"It's unfortunate, but it happens at universities and businesses all the time. He should have stepped down with people applauding him."

Although Toner did not leave at the top of his game and was a lightning rod for everything that ailed UConn athletics at the time, he nonetheless made some significant contributions toward the success the basketball programs are enjoying today. In addition to making the decision to join the Big East, he also hired Geno Auriemma and Jim Calhoun and was a force behind the construction of Gampel Pavilion.

"I think the task force report was an honest assessment of what they found," Meiser-McKnett says. "Obviously the report had to be directed toward the leadership, that's what made it go. That's what the task force was asked to do, lay some facts out on the line.

"The state of athletics at the University of Connecticut in 1985–86 was the result of an institution that did not know what it wanted to do with its own programs. You tell John Toner we want to be in the Top Three in the Big East Conference, that's a whole different ball game. What were the goals of the university? What were DiBiaggio's expectations for athletics? John was a very accommodating person. John was a team player within a university system. I can't be critical of John Toner because I'm not sure the university ever cared enough about athletics to say what they wanted."

In retrospect, Toner was a man caught in the headlights of transition. A new age was dawning at UConn and with it a new commitment to athletics, a new marketing strategy, a raised level of expectation. And the Magna Carta of this movement, the document that would set forth its guiding principles, was the President's Task Force Report on Athletics. Wielding the white paper like Excalibur, Casteen could now cut a swath through the inertia and make the sweeping changes that were necessary.

The Arrival of Jim Calhoun

Dom Perno's words of resignation were still hanging fresh in the air when the calls began coming in. Where do I get an application? Who do I send my résumé to? The college coaching fraternity is a tight lot, but it is a competitive, ambitious one as well. Granted, the University of Connecticut might be rapidly becoming "The Northwestern of the Big East," as one referee was heard to remark, but it was still a job in one of the nation's premiere basketball conferences.

Toner had formed a search committee the day after Perno's departure. It was charged with interviewing coaching candidates and making a recommendation; Toner would then make the final decision. President Casteen also indicated he might become involved in the final selection process. The committee was given a month to do its work.

Early candidates included Butch Beard, a former NBA

player; George Karl and Bob Zuffelato (a Torrington native), who had NBA coaching experience; Dave Bike, a respected coach at Sacred Heart University; and Bob Dukiet, a successful coach at St. Peter's. In a relatively short period of time, however, the list of candidates was pared down to three men: Mitch Buonaguro of Fairfield University, Nick Macarchuk of Canisius, and Jim Calhoun of Northeastern.

Buonaguro, thirty-two, had been an assistant at Villanova in 1985 when the Wildcats won the national championship. He had taken over at Fairfield and in his first season won the Metro Atlantic Athletic Conference, compiled a 26-4 record, got into the NCAA Tournament, and won just about every rookie Coach of the Year award. If there was a hot coach around, it was Buonaguro.

Macarchuk, forty-four, had turned around a flailing Canisius program that had been on NCAA probation nine years earlier. He was coming off a 20-8 season and a second-place finish to Northeastern in the Eastern Collegiate Athletic Conference North Atlantic Conference. Another thing Macarchuk had going for him was his hometown, nearby Norwich, Connecticut.

Calhoun was the most solid candidate of the group. In fourteen years at Northeastern, the forty-four-year-old Calhoun had a record of 250-137 and had taken his team to the NCAA Tournament in five of the six previous seasons. What made him even more appealing to UConn was that forty-seven of the fifty-two scholarship players Calhoun had recruited and coached at Northeastern had earned their degrees.

A few days after naming the search committee, Toner set

off on an exploration mission of his own. As a former, well-respected president of the NCAA, Toner had contacts all over the country. There was not a phone he couldn't ring. Toner may not have known who the best available coach was, but he knew the people who did. And the name he kept hearing over and over was Jim Calhoun.

Less than a week into the search for a new coach, Toner called Calhoun at Northeastern and asked him if he might be interested in the vacancy. Calhoun told him he didn't think so, but Toner persisted. He asked Calhoun to meet him at the Boar's Head Tavern in Sturbridge, Massachusetts, which is located about halfway between Storrs and Boston. Calhoun agreed.

"At that meeting, John asked what it would take to get me to Connecticut," Calhoun recalls. "I had the impression at the time that he had already decided that I was the guy he wanted."

Wanting Calhoun was one thing. Getting him was going to be quite another. Toner discovered that Calhoun wasn't planning on going anywhere. He had a very good team, led by Reggie Lewis. He was tenured at Northeastern and had already been promised he would be the next athletic director. In addition, he had been born and raised in the Greater Boston area and loved the city. All his family and his wife, Pat's, family lived there. He was comfortable, secure, and middle-aged, an often deadly combination when it comes to taking on new challenges.

That spring, Calhoun had done all his requisite professional midlife soul-searching when he had been offered the head coaching job at Northwestern of the Big Ten. He ended up not taking the lucrative job, in large part because of something Indiana coach Bob Knight had told him: "Knight told me that the Big Ten was a league of institutions, that the institutions win or lose, that if he left Indiana, Indiana would still win. So would Michigan. But Northwestern would always be bad."

Another consideration was the situation at Connecticut, where the team had just suffered its fourth straight losing season and was surely headed for a fifth. But two things gave Calhoun pause to reflect on the offer: He knew people were not going to keep knocking on his door if he continued to say no. And there was something alluring about the state of Connecticut and its relationship with the university's basketball team.

Calhoun had become intrigued with UConn at the Connecticut Mutual Classic the previous December. He had heard Perno talk about Connecticut basketball, the interest, the fanaticism, the media involvement. And when he attended a reception at the Hartford Club prior to the tournament, he had met Dee Rowe, Casteen, and others and gotten a sense of how important basketball was to the state. But he didn't fully understand the depth of the involvement until his Northeastern team played UConn in the championship game.

"About twelve thousand, thirteen thousand people showed up for the game," Calhoun says, "and the biggest thing that hit me was that they didn't care at all about us. We played terrific, we were up about thirty before Earl Kelley brought them back, but we still won by about fifteen.

"But afterward at the press conference every question was directed at UConn. They didn't care about Reggie Lewis.

They didn't care about any of my other kids, my coaching ability, all they cared about were the guys in blue and white. All Northeastern was, was the team that beat them. And there was this mass of media. I had been to other big press conferences at the NCAA Tournament—Syracuse, Virginia—but I had never experienced anything like this. I was taken aback by it. This was clearly different.

"It was like opening a door and walking into a room. It gave me a lot better understanding of what Dom had been talking about. The Connecticut Mutual Classic was a factor in me finally accepting the job because it gave me insight into how basketball could captivate this state. It was something you couldn't do in Boston. I remember calling [Syracuse coach] Jim Boeheim about the job, and he was one of the most positive people I talked to. He said the job had a lot of potential, that it was the closest thing in the conference to Syracuse in that it is the only show in town. He thought I could get all the attention I wanted, all the television, and that kids would feel good about coming here to play."

Over the next several weeks, Toner and Calhoun continued to talk. Toner, the old-school athletic director severely criticized in the task force report, was under pressure himself. Landing Calhoun, he believed, would be a big step in the direction of job security.

If UConn was going to get Calhoun, the university was going to have to let some of the moths out of the old wallet. Calhoun was adamant about being paid commensurate with other Big East coaches, and the salary on the table was significantly less than what Calhoun had been offered at Northwestern or even Duquesne the previous year. More important to

Calhoun than money, however, was length of contract. He felt it was going to take some time to turn things around, and he wanted the security if things didn't work out.

"Back before Rollie Massimino took the Las Vegas [head coach] job, I was one of the people that was contacted," Calhoun explains. "They told me when everything was said and done I would make eight hundred thousand dollars a year. Well, that makes you sit up and take notice. You say to yourself, maybe that's four or five years of misery, but even if I don't do well in March, that's still four or five million dollars. So if you are unsuccessful, you still have a pretty good nest egg to go find something you can be successful at."

Another important consideration for Calhoun was the chance for success. UConn was now at the bottom of the Big East ladder. How many rungs up could Calhoun realistically expect to climb? One thing any new coach coming into the conference definitely had going for him was its relative newness. Whereas the Big Ten was a conference of institutions, the Big East was a conference of coaches, a league in which the men with the most dominant personalities emerged with the best programs.

"Every job should be evaluated on who you are going to pass in the league," Calhoun says. "If a new school comes into the Big Ten, who are they going to pass? It's like the three new schools coming into the Big East this year. It's not whether they are going to be any good, the question is, who are they going to go by. Take the ACC. I talked to Rick Barnes before he took his job at Clemson. He wondered, 'Is the best we are ever going to be able to do here fourth or fifth?' No one takes over a job to do that. They take over a program to be the best they can be.

"I looked around the league and thought there were a lot of good things here. The state has three million people, is the wealthiest state in the union, and there is nowhere else in the conference with the exception of Syracuse where you can captivate the entire state. I mean, the last game Dom Perno ever coached here, they sold out the Hartford Civic Center."

Another factor was the task force report, which Calhoun had seen before it was made public. Although the report has always been widely credited as being a major element in Calhoun's decision-making process, in fact, it was not.

"The task force was important to me in that people were aware that things had to be changed," Calhoun says. "We had to get into the nineties. I thought the report was more of an initiator of an attitude than anything else. It was something that made me feel better about coming here because it made the university look at itself and realize it needed to make some changes. Anytime you have self-evaluation, in this case public self-evaluation, then I think you are on the right track.

"In my contract I used some of the language from the task force as a means of implementation. It said for me to be successful, you have to do certain things. It also made it easy for me at some point to go back and say, you guys said you were screwed up. As it turned out I didn't have to do that, but it was there.

"Was it a factor in my decision? Yes. But if we were only going to draw three thousand people, it would have been no factor at all. If we didn't have a great recruiting base in the state, it would have been no factor at all."

Interestingly, the task force report didn't mean much to Auriemma, either. "I knew how those things are," Auriemma says. "Somebody could just throw that thing in a trash can, or a new president could come in and say, hey, forget it, we're staying just where we are, or we'll implement it in the next ten to fifteen years. Well, that doesn't do me any good.

"I went to this kid's house to recruit after the report came out, and I talked about new buildings, new facilities, everything that was going on. And her father said to me, 'Coach, I hate to burst your bubble, but my son graduated from Fairfield two years ago, and when UConn was recruiting *him*, he was supposed to play in that building.'

"So to me, it was just forget about everything else. Go out, get good kids, coach the hell out of them. Try to sell the program any way we can. That task force report didn't mean anything to me."

Chris Dailey, however, saw the task force report as a benefit in recruiting. "I remember there was this kid I had been close to at Rutgers," Dailey says, "and she contacted me. She was a terrific player, but I told Geno we weren't ready for her because she would need a lot more support academically than we could give her. Early on, there were at-risk kids that we were unable to recruit.

"The task force made a commitment to student athletes. It made a statement on the quality of life for student athletes and the retention of student athletes. It really helped because it put a big emphasis on what student athletes were experiencing, more than just basketball, the whole picture."

If Calhoun had not taken the job, the search committee might have played a larger role in the selection process. But when Calhoun met with the committee, he knew he was clearly the front-runner. Still, Toner had told Calhoun he wanted him to have the committee's "blessing."

"When you are hiring a coach you look for a match," Meiser-McKnett, a search committee member, says. "But the truth was, we didn't have much to offer, were ninth in the conference. We did have the Big East, but that was essentially it. All you had to do was walk inside the Field House for five minutes to see how things were."

After Calhoun met with the committee, Toner took a straw vote to see who their preference would be. Calhoun was the winner.

"The thing that comes across loud and clear when you meet Jim Calhoun is his strength," Meiser-McKnett says. "He was in control, and it was clear that we were going to have to recruit him. He impressed me as a man who knew what he wanted to do. He was very focused, very intense. And I liked that. The next coach had to be somebody strong. If anything was going to happen at Connecticut, it was going to take someone who was willing to raise hell. Jim is a very, very bright guy, and he knows how to make things work for him. He is very focused, and you better be ready to think when you talk to him or he will outsmart you."

Although Calhoun was approaching the UConn job as if he were 100 percent sure he would take it if it were offered, in truth, he had very serious misgivings about leaving Northeastern and his beloved Boston. He would not make up his mind until the very last minute and even then would not feel secure for some time that he had made the right decision.

On Monday, May 12, six days before the May 18 deadline

Toner had set for having a new coach in place, Calhoun met with Casteen, who was interviewing the final three candidates. The two sat down to breakfast, and Casteen's first question was short and to the point: "Tell me how to build a basketball program." Casteen, who stayed behind the scenes, was impressed with Calhoun. On Tuesday, Toner offered Calhoun the job, but Calhoun put him off until Wednesday. He spent Tuesday night at home in Dedham, Massachusetts, with his wife, Pat, talking about things, trying to make sure all the possibilities, all the variables had been covered. He still had not decided.

On Wednesday, Calhoun received another call from Toner and told him he needed one more night to sleep on it. In the afternoon, he met with Jack Curry, an executive vice president at Northeastern, for three hours, at which point one of three counteroffers was made. He also received a call from the president of Northeastern, who asked what he could do to keep Calhoun. That night, he met with his players at Northeastern and told them he had not made a decision. Later he went to an awards banquet, at which many friends and colleagues from Northeastern were in attendance, to receive a coaching honor.

"I had a very tough time making my mind up," Calhoun says. "I'd say I probably accepted and turned the job down in my mind about ten or twelve times. I'll bet I told myself no fifteen times."

On Thursday morning at 8 A.M., Calhoun called Toner and told him he would take the job. In Calhoun, UConn was getting a man who believed in hard work, rebounding, pressing defense, fast-break offense, and athleticism over height.

The school was also getting a man who had been a winner everywhere he had ever played or coached.

Before leaving Boston for Storrs, Calhoun met individually with each of his Northeastern players. He also made a few phone calls inquiring about some possible recruits who might still be available. Then he got into his car and headed west on the Mass Pike toward the biggest challenge of his professional life.

"I am delighted that Mr. Calhoun has accepted the position of head basketball coach," Casteen announced. "He was selected from an extraordinary group of finalists for his demonstrated capacity to build and to lead and for his commitment to the fundamental concept that educational excellence is the first mission of a successful program."

Calhoun was introduced in late afternoon to a jam-packed press conference as the seventeenth men's basketball coach in the school's history. "By the end of the press conference I couldn't speak," Calhoun says. "I felt like I had talked to everyone in the world. It was a very long day."

Calhoun's agreement with the university called for seven years. But, he says, it was divided into two parts: "I had three years to get us right and four years to win. I called a friend of mine and told him, if it takes that long, they will buy me out. I knew the honeymoon wouldn't last that long, but, psychologically, coming from a tenured position with a promise to be the next athletic director, I needed it."

Calhoun did not feel the full impact of what he had done until Saturday morning when he awakened at about 5 A.M. and realized he was not the Northeastern coach anymore. "It was my hardest morning," he says. "I called a friend of mine.

He said, you're not having second thoughts, and I said not really second thoughts, but it happened kind of quick because I really didn't make my mind up until I called John on Thursday. He asked, you're going, aren't you? And I said I'm going. And he said you're just calling me to reassure yourself that it's all right. And I said yeah. He said we would take you back tomorrow, take you back yesterday, but you don't belong back here. I guess I needed someone neutral to say it was all right."

Later that morning, Calhoun and his two sons, Jim and Jeff, went over to his office at Northeastern and packed fourteen years of memories into plain cardboard boxes. On Sunday morning, Jim and Pat Calhoun took a plane to Puerto Rico, where the Big East meetings were being held.

"I'll always remember we got into our room, and probably for the first time we slowed down. And I said something like, holy shit, what did we get ourselves into. And we looked at each other and just started laughing."

Jim Calhoun:
Hard Work and *More* Hard Work

Henry Payne, who played basketball at American International College in Springfield, Massachusetts, in the early 1960s, remembers one of his teammates, Jim Calhoun, this way: "He was one of those guys who was always bleeding. He was always on the floor, always diving for loose balls." In two sentences, Payne's recollection sums up the athlete-coach-competitor side of the University of Connecticut head basketball coach: intensity and hard work, dirty work and intensity, intensity and more hard work.

As a player, the Boston Irish blue-collar ethic served Calhoun well, earning the six-foot-five forward Little All-American honors. As a coach in his twenty-fourth year as the head of a college program, it has placed him at the top of his profession. As a person, it almost got him killed once.

True story:

Calhoun is coaching at Northeastern University in Boston. He leaves the office late one night. He is walking to his car when a guy with a knife comes out of the shadows and tells Calhoun to hand over his wallet. Calhoun tells the punk to do something that is anatomically impossible. They scuffle. Calhoun gets slashed on the hand, but he subdues the mugger, administering some vigilante justice in the process. The police come. The attacker is greatly relieved. "He went to the hospital, I went to the hospital, but he didn't get my wallet," Calhoun says. "Someone else's reaction might have been to run. Someone else might have just given him the wallet. My reaction was, well, stupid."

On the sidelines, Calhoun doesn't give up anything without a fight either. Tie loose, jacket open, shirttail sometimes trailing, he works the area in front of the UConn bench with a panhandler's sense of mission. Arms folded, he glares at players. Palms turned upward, he implores the gods. Face reddening, he barks off-color critiques to passing officials. "If you ever get nervous during games," Calhoun likes to tell luncheon audiences, "just watch me. I'll be a calming influence."

But there is more than fire and brimstone to the fifty-four-year-old Bostonian. Calhoun the man is as different from Calhoun the coach as are a rebounder and somebody on the rebound.

"Jim has a great strength about him," says his wife, Pat, "as well as a great gentleness." The two met on a blind date arranged by one of Calhoun's sisters. "He was funny, easy to talk to," Pat recalls. "I think it was his humor that attracted me to him."

Another facet of Calhoun's personality, which those who

view him only in a basketball venue might find surprising, is shyness. "It takes him a long time to be comfortable with people in a social situation," Pat says. "That's just his nature. He's been that way since he was a kid. Sometimes people think he is aloof, and I can understand how you could perceive that, but it's wrong."

As a father, Calhoun is and was always very close to their two now grown sons, James, twenty-eight, and Jeff, twenty-three. When they were small, he would often come home late and wake them up just so they could share some time. "He has always been a better father than I have been a mother, and I say that with all sincerity," Pat says. "When the kids were small, it was always Jim they seemed to go to. He always had a gift for that. I can count on one hand the number of times he ever even raised his voice to the kids."

Out in the driveway, in "friendly" one-on-one games, the Calhoun boys did, however, get a glimpse of dad the competitor. Even though he was a high school basketball star and scholarship player at UConn for two years, Jeff Calhoun never beat his father. "He played me very physically," Jeff says. "Basically, I wasn't going to get an open shot."

Jimmy Calhoun was fifteen years old, playing center field for the local Babe Ruth team in Braintree, Massachusetts, when the game was suddenly stopped and a man Calhoun didn't know walked out to him. The conversation was awkward, brief:

"You have to come with me."

"Why?"

"Your father's dead."

Calhoun was devastated. He and his father had also been

close. Still, when he got home, he told his mother not to worry: "I'll take care of you."

It didn't take long for things to get tough for the family of four girls, two boys, and no father. But they stuck together. "It was a hardworking environment," says Joan Girard, Calhoun's younger sister. "Everyone had to pull their own weight. Being the oldest boy, Jim probably had to pull more than his share."

"My father was always the one people turned to," Calhoun says. "I got that from him. I learned that responsibility wasn't something to be backed away from."

One of the obligations Calhoun assumed was to his brother, Billy, who was four when their father died of a massive heart attack. "In a lot of ways, Jim acted like a surrogate father," Bill Calhoun, now a cardiologist in Boston, says. "We did a lot of things together."

In addition to helping raise his brother, working at odd jobs, and going to school, Calhoun also starred in football, basketball, and baseball at Braintree High School. He won a basketball scholarship to AIC and left for college in the fall of 1961. But by mid-October, he had to quit school and move back home because the family was having a hard time. Billy was nine, two of his sisters were in school, and his mother's health wasn't good.

He got a job in North Quincy cutting gravestones. It was hard, physical work, but the money was good and each week he gave two thirds of what he earned to his mother. "It was discouraging at times," he says, "but I learned some hard and positive lessons about life and what I had to do."

The following year he returned to AIC, where he earned a

reputation as a good shooter, fierce rebounder, and strong competitor. Besides playing basketball and studying, he also held down part-time jobs, one of which was washing the team's uniforms after games. "Off the court, Jim was very popular," ex-teammate Payne says. "He knew more about basketball than anyone: stats, who the starting players were for other teams. And he was very witty, very sharp. He always drew a crowd."

Calhoun led AIC in scoring his last two years. He was team captain his senior year and helped the team to an NCAA Division II play-off berth. He left there as the school's fourth all-time leading scorer.

After graduating from AIC in 1968 with a degree in sociology, Calhoun remained at the school for two years as an assistant coach. In 1968, he took a job coaching basketball at Old Lyme High School in Connecticut, where, he says, he learned that "just playing hard wasn't enough. You had to perform technically too."

Following a year at Old Lyme, Calhoun moved to Westport High School in New Bedford, Massachusetts, and then upstate to Dedham High School, where his team was 21-1 in 1971–72 and reached the state semifinals. Following this season, he was a surprise choice to coach the Northeastern Huskies. One of the people who had recommended him for the job, without Calhoun's knowledge, was Celtics legend Red Auerbach.

Calhoun took over a Division II program at Northeastern and transformed it into one that was nationally recognized on the Division I level. In fourteen seasons, his record was 250-137, and in five of his last six seasons, Northeastern received invitations to the NCAA Tournament. His teams also dominated the newly formed ECAC North Atlantic Conference, and for his accomplishments Calhoun received several Coach of the Year awards.

Not surprisingly, hustle and grit were earmarks of Calhoun's Northeastern teams. The style of play included a fast-breaking offense, pressing defense, and a fanatical dedication to rebounding. Despite never having a truly big man, Northeastern won the national Division I rebounding title three times.

In putting together his teams at Northeastern, Calhoun established himself as a sound judge of talent. Unable to get the blue-chip players, Calhoun developed an eye for athletic players who would fit into his system. The late Reggie Lewis, who became a star with the Boston Celtics, was probably his most celebrated find. But during the course of his tenure at Northeastern, Calhoun had five players drafted by the NBA.

Although the end result was something to behold, the process of becoming a "Jim Calhoun team" was taxing. The occasional midnight practice session and regular boot-camp conditioning drills became part of the Calhoun lore at Northeastern. Players soon learned that their coach did not take well to losing and that life was better all around when they were posting more points on the scoreboard than the opposition. "We were coming back from New Hampshire," recalls Pete Harris, a former leading scorer at Northeastern. "We had lost, and as we were getting off the bus he said to us, 'You've got thirty minutes to get ready for practice.' Now that made everybody real happy. . . . At first you say, who is this madman? Then you see what he's trying to do and how he's trying to help you. He kind of grows on you."

When UConn athletic director John Toner came courting Calhoun, he didn't have much to offer. But he knew his man. Instead of waving around dollar bills and promises, Toner appealed to Calhoun's competitive instincts.

"When John Toner offered me the job, I had reservations," Calhoun says. "I still had Reggie Lewis and another Top Twenty team and all that. But Toner told me to evaluate from the standpoint of what I would like to end up doing competitively. That was the first time I started looking at it differently. He said he knew I could do well at the next level. And wouldn't I like to be there competitively. I went out on one of my runs along the Charles River, and I started thinking about it."

In a second meeting, Toner planted the final seed. "He reminded me that I went to a high school situation in Dedham where people said I couldn't win and my team won twenty-one straight my last year," Calhoun says. "He reminded me that when I went to Northeastern the school was Division Two and when I left it was the best team in New England. I realized that he was flattering me. But he was being thought-provoking as well. He had me thinking, do I want to wake up one morning four years from now saying I had a chance to compete at a different level and turned it down? Anybody who knows me understands that if you appeal to my competitive aspect, it's hard for me to resist."

When Calhoun ultimately decided to take the job at UConn, many who knew him questioned whether he would be able to handle the losing that most certainly would come as he struggled to establish the program.

"He'll continue to be a bad loser," Jack Grinold, Northeastern's sports information director and one of Calhoun's close friends, predicted after Calhoun took the UConn job. "He doesn't like it. He won't run and hide in the closet. He won't hold it in. I don't mean he will blame his players. But he will cuss the world like Ahab. He's one of God's great Irishmen."

And curse the world Calhoun did, along with his players, assistants, officials, and anyone else who stood in the way of winning. UConn basketball fans certainly were used to seeing animated coaches on the sidelines. Since the formation of the Big East Conference, they had enjoyed the anguish of St. John's Lou Carnesecca, heckled Villanova's Rollie Massimino and his histrionics, scowled back at Georgetown's John Thompson and his menacing hulk. But never had they seen one of their own walk the sidelines with the holy fervor of Jim Calhoun. And while many simply assumed they were watching the pressure-induced ravings of a man under too much strain, there was, in fact, a method behind the apparent madness.

"Early on, did I believe that the officials would call something for Georgetown simply because it was Georgetown? The answer is yes," Calhoun says. "Georgetown would play physical defense and get away with it. Connecticut would play physically and get whistled. So when I came here I had to fight. It's like if I went to listen to a baritone, I might ask my wife, was he really good? If I go to see Pavarotti, I don't have to ask if he is good, I assume he is good. The point is, once you get there you don't have to tell people to respect you, they just do.

"And I think the first couple of years, the officials understood. When we got better, I had to adjust. I remember one official telling me, 'Okay, Jim, you're up fourteen, get off our asses, we're doing a good job.' And he was right. It's just that everyone in the league used to say nice things about Dom Perno, about what a great guy he was. I didn't want Rollie Massimino and John Thompson saying nice things about me."

While Calhoun has no second thoughts about his game demeanor in the early days—in one two-season stretch he picked up thirteen technicals—he does regret the public perception. Particularly disturbing to some was the manner in which Calhoun would dress down or chastise players. At one point, the parents of players were permanently moved from their seats behind the bench to the opposite side of the court so they could be spared Calhoun's often spicy tirades.

"How intense would you be if you had to perform all the work you do in a year in just sixty hours?" Calhoun says. "What the public saw of me was a snapshot. But life is a motion picture. It continues to roll. While they saw me drive, push, prod a kid to be the best he can be, they never saw the other twenty-two hours of association I have with him."

Calhoun employs a good cop–bad cop approach to dealing with his players, and he plays both roles. He is, at once, surrogate parent, teacher, friend, and father confessor. And always, he is demanding. On recruiting visits he tells the parents of players: "When I come into your home, I am coming to take your son away. He is now in my care. I promise you, no one is going to ask more of him for three hundred and sixty-five days of the year, for four years, in a lifetime."

If work is the trait that defines Calhoun, it also is the trademark of his teams. "Every team thinks it is in good condition, and every team thinks it plays hard, and they do," Calhoun says. "But no one plays as hard as we do." And they don't.

Calhoun's practices are not the screaming, ball-kicking, clipboard-skipping affairs one might imagine, although all of these things do take place from time to time. Rather, they are structured, intense sessions that Calhoun uses to teach and prepare. The outbursts are few and far between, and when they do come they are often more a product of design than temper. A constant technique is profanity, which Calhoun often employs for effect. Come over here, please, and get the bleep over here produce different reactions, not to mention response times.

"A coach who takes the license to really push his kids has to earn that license," Calhoun says. "The most important thing I have to do is to get them to know how much I really care about them. I couldn't act the way I do if I didn't really care about them."

"Jim always had a great concept of family, and he pulls that over the entire team," Grinold says. "It is something that works for him, but it is also sincere. The feeling comes out of Jim, it isn't a philosophy out of the Harvard Business School."

"Jim sees his role as a teacher, and he takes it very seriously," Pat Calhoun says. "He knows he is touching their lives. He doesn't see his role as being for just the four years.

His highest aspirations for his players isn't as basketball players, it's as people."

In that vein, Calhoun tries to broaden his players whenever possible. On the road, it is a common practice to take a team side trip to some nearby historical site or museum. The team also often dines in ethnic restaurants for the cultural experience. While those who have played for Calhoun agree the experience was not always pleasant, almost to a man they admit it helped make them better people and more able to deal with life in the real world.

Calhoun himself has mellowed some over the past several years. Some attribute this to having better teams, thus having less to become upset about. But it goes deeper than that. "I'm constantly evaluating my relationship with my players," Calhoun says. "Am I pushing too hard, am I not pushing hard enough? . . . I think I have gotten to the point that I don't want to embarrass the kids. A couple of kids didn't handle it well. I still get on them, but not the same way. I think I relate well to the kids. What's the difference between me and Kevin Ollie? My dad died when I was young. I grew up in a city, he grew up in a city. He didn't have a lot, I didn't have a lot."

In fact, it is his relationship with his players that Calhoun says keeps him involved in coaching: "I never thought I could ever like anyone as much as Steve Pikiell or Tate George. Then Lyman DePriest came along, and then Kevin Ollie, and so on. The ability to work with kids, to see them get better and to win, keeps me motivated. And I like the university setting. I like the smell of spring. I like the fall when the students come back. I love the game. I love having a team. I love overcoming obstacles."

Calhoun still manages to fill his days with a schedule that would stagger a normal person. But he says he spends his timedifferently now. Instead of battling the administration over academics or facilities, he now fills his time by involving himself with a wide array of charitable organizations, including Ronald McDonald Houses, the American Cancer Society, Homeward Bound Foundation of Hartford, and Big Brothers/Big Sisters.

After twenty-eight years as a coach, he says there are moments, particularly in the weeks after a season ends, that he gets tired, has a letdown. But it doesn't last because there is always a kid that wants to talk, a recruit who needs to be visited, another battle to be fought, another season just around the corner.

Rebuilding:
The Men's Program

Following his whirlwind courtship by UConn and heady reception in Puerto Rico as the newest member of the Big East coaching fraternity, Jim Calhoun returned to the Storrs campus—and reality.

He was inheriting a program that was coming off four straight losing seasons.

He was taking over a team with only seven scholarship players.

He was going to have to recruit in the wake of the Earl Kelley embarrassment.

He was being forced to operate in a glass house with curious noses pressed against every pane.

And he was being asked to turn around a program without the aid of first-class facilities or support services.

Four days into his new job, it all hit home. Calhoun awoke

one morning to the horrible realization that he might have made a huge mistake in taking the UConn job. While going through the hiring process, Calhoun had been struck by how desperately many people wanted to turn around UConn's basketball fortunes. Firsthand, at the Connecticut Mutual Classic the previous December, he had seen the depth of feeling UConn basketball generated and the tremendous media and fan interest. But now, in his first week on the job, he was encountering a segment of the university community that not only had little interest in trying to accommodate athletics but was downright hostile to the very concept.

"All of a sudden," Calhoun says, "I was walking into places and meeting people who were saying, 'No, that's not the way it's going to be.' "

With Toner guiding him through the university bureaucracy, Calhoun doggedly set about the task of getting his message across. There were no dead spots in his twelve-hour-a-day routine. Whether it was one course, one issue, one professor, one department head at a time, Calhoun made the same point over and over: Academic success for his players was important to him, and it was in the student athletes' best interest, the university's best interest, and Calhoun's best interest.

"I had to convince people that from a business standpoint alone, I wanted kids to graduate," Calhoun says. "That if I recruited a kid from Detroit and that kid didn't graduate, then I couldn't go back to Detroit. The other battle was trying to make the rest of the university understand that we should be part of the university, that we were really nothing more than the front porch of a great mansion. When I was being hired, some people asked me if I was planning to bring in any potential professional players and I told them, we are not a franchise, we are a university. The battles were unbelievable, and I would walk over and have to fight them every single day."

Pat Meiser-McKnett says the sheer force of Calhoun's personality was the most important ingredient in dealing with the mind-set. "Jim took his players, his coaches, and his program and assumed responsibility for what happened in their lives," she says. "And that meant sitting down with the director of admissions, counselors, faculty. He basically came in and said we are going to deal with things directly, and that is what he did. An athletic department needs to communicate all the time, tell its story because there are so many misconceptions about college athletics. It doesn't necessarily have to be your basketball coach doing this, but in that particular situation, Jim was the guy."

Slowly, in baby-step increments, Calhoun made progress, though the journey was often one step forward, two back. The academic coordinator for athletics, who was responsible under the old system for up to five hundred athletes, was replaced. The Counseling Program for Intercollegiate Athletics was formed, and an energetic woman named Joy O'Shields was hired to run it.

Then it was found that the academic coordinator to men's basketball was not relating to the players well, and he was replaced. Calhoun was able to push Ruth Mead, an academic counselor who also had been a head coach of both women's volleyball and softball at UConn, into the position. And while Mead finally proved to be the right person, she was still the third academic coordinator the men's basketball program had in Calhoun's first semester.

While academics were his primary battle, an adversary that would come back to blindside him at midseason, it was not the only brawl in town. Every day there would be little skirmishes over matters such as meal money for the players, among the lowest in the Big East, or getting a bus with a bathroom, or having that bus drop the players off at their dorms rather than the Field House at 2 A.M. And then, of course, there was the little matter of recruiting, the very key to existence. "I can't tell you how hard we worked trying to get the right kids," Calhoun says. "We did everything we could." The result was six new recruits, including Lyman DePriest from the Detroit area, Willie McCloud from Maryland, and Murray Williams from Torrington.

Because Calhoun had been hired after the spring semester ended, his first meeting with his players didn't come until the first day of classes in September. Calhoun's major objective from a purely basketball perspective was to establish a work ethic. His goal was to field a team that might not outplay conference opponents but would never be outworked by any of them. The conditioning program Calhoun outlined at the meeting was the first step. It called for lifting weights Monday, Wednesday, and Friday, running the other four days, and practicing basketball every day. "The other day you can have off," Calhoun told the team.

A sight that would soon become common at Storrs was the entire team running up and down a half-mile hill in the campus cemetery. And not just once or twice but ten times. By the time official practices began in mid-October, the team was not only in shape but already close as a unit. But as well conditioned as the players were, it still did not prepare them for the first practice.

Calhoun opened the season by closing the first half of practice to the media. Tiny Guyer Gym was selected for the initial player-coach gathering for a very simple reason: It is easier to hold someone's attention if you are meeting him in a closet as opposed to a three-ring circus. The session featured lots of running, lots of hustle, lots of red-faced, in-your-face intensity. And when the one-hour, fifteen-minute introduction to Exhaustion 101 was over, the message Calhoun wished to send had been received loud and clear.

"It was the hardest practice I've ever been through," junior Jeff King said afterward.

"No way we could have done it without the conditioning program," senior Gerry Besselink said. "There would have to be buckets set up all around the court."

For freshman guard Tate George, the biggest impression had not been made by the grueling workout. It had been made by Calhoun. "I've never had a coach come in my face and tell me how he feels," George said. "It happened five or six times. I'll have to use some better judgment."

Calhoun's assessment was somewhat different: "We didn't want to work them too hard," he said. "Today was a good day for introductions."

Although UConn went into the season opener ready to do battle, it quickly became apparent that while they were gung-ho, they had few weapons. After squeezing past UMass, they lost to Yale, managed a ten-point victory over Central Connecticut, and got thumped by Purdue. Then the team boarded a bus for Boston on the afternoon of December 10 to play Boston University, beginning one of the more bizarre road trips in UConn history.

Before the day was over, the UConn bus would be involved in a serious accident on the sleet-slicked Massachusetts Turnpike. BU officials would refuse to cancel the game, which would eventually start at 9:45 P.M. The contest would feature a bench-clearing brawl, arguments over TV time-outs and the score, and end at 11:56 P.M. with a UConn loss.

A month following the BU follies, UConn would be involved in another collision, a head-on crash between athletics and academics, a mishap that would prove much more injurious to the basketball program. In late August, Cliff Robinson and Phil Gamble, UConn's two true Big East–caliber players, had done well enough in summer school courses to be ruled eligible for the fall semester. In the absence of academic counseling, Calhoun had helped tutor them personally. While there was relief over the news of their reinstatement, those close to the program knew there was still cause for concern because the university's policy regarding grade point averages was unchanged.

In essence, that policy mandated that students be placed on academic probation if they failed to meet the following minimum standards: 1.6 GPA the first semester, 1.8 semester or cumulative GPA after two semesters, 1.9 semester or cumulative GPA after three semesters, and 2.0 semester or cumulative GPA after four semesters.

Although Robinson and Gamble had met the semester GPA requirement of 1.9 following their third semester, they had not received high-enough grades to pull their overall

averages up enough to comply with the cumulative requirements. Thus, while both Robinson and Gamble had semester
GPAs above 2.0, they were still mere tenths of a point away
from achieving the necessary 1.9 cumulative score.

"Cliff and Phil were almost doomed to fail before the semester started," Calhoun says. "They were not only operat-
ing under a dual-edged sword, the GPA and the cumulative,
but they were also taking exceptionally hard courses. They
had done poorly Dom's last semester, and when I came, people told me, 'Well, we'll put them in the right courses.' But
they *didn't* put them in the right courses."

The situation reminded Calhoun of a conversation he had
had with Syracuse coach Jim Boeheim in Puerto Rico right
after taking the UConn job: "We're walking on the beach and
Boeheim says, 'John Toner needs you because it has been
tough for him the past few years, so he will stick by you. And
the university won't allow anything bad to happen because
they had the kids flunk out last year.' Now, sure as hell, here
they were setting themselves up to do it all over again."

Of course, Boeheim was unfamiliar with just how bad the
situation was at UConn. Over the preceding years, the university had admitted as many as ten very marginal students because they played basketball. Those students had Scholastic
Aptitude Test scores in the five hundred to seven hundred
range, while the mean at the time was a score of almost 1,050.

Robinson and Gamble learned of their failure in early January, but under university rules they would remain eligible
until the start of the second semester on January 27. In the
two-week interim, Calhoun, characteristically, fought. "We finally had this twenty-three-person meeting in John Casteen's

office," he says. "A lot of research had been done to show how the system was unfair and how the kids were taking wrong courses.

"I had been led to believe going into the meeting that we had a chance because of the extenuating circumstances. But when I got there, I knew we were in trouble. What it came down to was politics; no one wanted to take charge of the situation. The appeals process actually came down to someone taking out a calculator and readding the grades. I said, you people aren't educators, you're accountants. People there looked around, and they knew I was right. I said I agree we have to have standards, but we put these kids through grave jeopardy their freshman year and that was unfair."

The day following a loss to Providence on January 24, Robinson, the team's leading scorer, and Gamble, third in scoring, were publicly declared ineligible. The team was 6-10 overall and 1-6 in the Big East at the time. With its two best players gone, UConn won only three games the rest of the season.

"What losing Phil and Cliff showed was that you can hire any coach you want, but if you don't have a solid system of academic support, you're going to lose kids," Calhoun says. "And when you lose your two best kids at midseason and you have a brand-new coach, it's not the coach. There's something else wrong."

The night the appeal was lost, Calhoun, Meiser-McKnett, and Tim Tolokan, the associate athletic director for communications, sat around in Tolokan's kitchen until the early morning hours. Calhoun was down, Meiser-McKnett reduced to tears at one point. "I remember Jim asking at one point if we would have to forfeit the rest of the season if we didn't have enough players," Tolokan says. "It was probably the low point for Jim and his program."

Calhoun went to Robinson and Gamble and asked them to remain at UConn. Both, especially Robinson, could have gone elsewhere, and few would have blamed them. But each agreed to stay. "I think that was an early turning point for us," Calhoun says.

As might be imagined, the outcry among the UConn faithful was loud and shrill. How could this happen again? There was even talk that perhaps UConn did not belong in the Big East and should, instead, return to a Yankee Conference–caliber schedule. Calhoun dealt with the uproar in his usual manner: directly.

"I'll never forget, we were producing our own coach's TV show at the time in the basement of one of the buildings," Tolokan says, "and Jim went on the air and articulated the situation. He guaranteed both players would be back. You have to understand, there was no reason at the time to believe the two would be back. Connecticut had a long track record of losing players to academics, and once they were lost they never came back."

The nightmare season played out as one might expect, with one notable exception. In the second-to-last game, after UConn had fought and clawed its way to a two-point victory over Seton Hall, a crowd of eight thousand plus at the Hartford Civic Center called the team back onto the floor and gave them a standing ovation.

The question was why? The previous year, Dom Perno had been booed and berated at this juncture, and yet here was

Calhoun's team being applauded. Were these people not aware that the team's record was 9-19, that only three Big East games had been won, that again the star players had been lost to academics during the season?

"I think people understood that recruits were on the way and that things were going to get better," Calhoun says. "Also, I don't think there was a Rotary Club or Grange or alumni association in the state that I did not speak to, telling them to be patient, that UConn was a great institution and we were working hard on the problems."

The season also was important in that it instilled a work ethic in the players along with the intangibles important to success. And no shortcuts had been taken, no influx of junior college kids called upon to provide short-term success.

"After the season, Gerry Besselink came up to me and said it was the best basketball year of his life," Calhoun says. "And that was after we had gone nine and nineteen, so I knew the kids were buying what we were trying to sell."

Although many battles remained to be fought, several had been won:

The faculty senate softened the requirements applied to grade point averages, thereby making it easier for student athletes to be successful academically.

Casteen found $130,000 to spruce up the Field House and another $110,000 for the academic counseling program.

Murray Williams, a top state high school player, was recruited, thus mending some local fences, while nationally, the signing of Lyman DePriest helped gain a foothold in the valuable Detroit region.

Essential amenities such as more meal money for players

and better travel arrangements were obtained, and the athletic department hired its first full-time doctor.

While none of the gains were huge, dramatic victories, each was significant, each was an important small step, and each contributed to the unexpected giant stride the men's basketball program would take the following season.

Winning the NIT

While much of the foundation upon which Connecticut basketball would ultimately rise was being quietly, methodically put into place behind the scenes, two very public building blocks were added in the summer of 1987.

Ground was finally broken for the long-promised campus sports complex.

And William T. "Todd" Turner took over as athletic director.

After Casteen had finessed John Toner from office in January, he began looking for someone who could move the UConn athletic department into the 1990s. Eventually, he hired Turner, whom he had known at the University of Virginia and whose expertise included sports information, tickets, marketing, and promotion.

Just as Calhoun would prove to be the right person to lead

men's basketball from the court of mediocrity, Turner quickly showed he possessed the qualities UConn needed in an athletic director. He was knowledgeable, savvy, aggressive, well organized, and familiar with institutional politics as they involved athletics. "I don't want to be a caretaker at this point in my life," Turner said after being hired. "I saw it as a job that afforded a lot of potential for some creative challenges."

On the business side, Turner's priorities included a five-year program that would maximize revenue from gate receipts, television, and fund-raising. He advocated raising money by applying donations toward scholarships rather than development, believing people would contribute more if approached that way.

On the academic front, his stated goals were to "first graduate students and second gain the trust of the university community."

On the political hustings, he sounded very much like Calhoun: "One of my jobs is going to be to try and convince the university community that athletics is not here to bring discredit to the university. Rather, it is here to represent the university with dignity, style, and class and be a window to all good things that the university is."

Although they shared a philosophy and goals, Calhoun had mixed feelings about his boss. "I never got along with him personally, and I don't know how long I could have worked with him over a period of time," Calhoun says. "I found him cold and elitist with his management team. But in fairness, this was his first time around the block, and he meets me, strong personality, and I've been doing some of the things he wants to do now, and he doesn't want me in those areas, and he's right about that, and, well . . ."

From a strictly professional perspective, Calhoun gives Turner his due: "He was a great bureaucrat, a great organizer, and in a cold, calculated, bureaucratic way, he brought us into the nineties. He streamlined things and made us well functioning. And he bridged all the gaps. He wasn't necessarily good to his coaches or close to the athletes, but he systematically organized the department. On a short-term basis, he was probably very good for the university."

Meiser-McKnett credits the odd-couple combo of Turner and Calhoun as a major factor in turning things around. "Todd did the really big, broad things that needed to be done to bring the university back together and the athletes back into the university," she says. "And Jim did the same thing, except he did it in terms of men's basketball."

Tim Tolokan saw Turner's relationship with Casteen as being a key. "Todd had good management skills, and he got involved in everything," Tolokan says, "but what he really brought with him was a close working relationship with the president. He had the ear of John Casteen, and everyone knew it."

Geno Auriemma, in direct contrast to Calhoun, liked Turner on a personal level, considering him a friend. But he quickly learned that friendship was not going to be a factor in their professional relationship.

"When Todd came here we suddenly had someone with a frame of reference on what it takes to be successful," Auriemma says. "Turner went to North Carolina, and he worked at Virginia. So now you have a guy that when you walk into his office he looks at you and says I understand what you are saying. I know exactly what you are talking about. That was different from 'We've never done things that way here before. We can't envision that.' "

As Auriemma soon discovered, there was a significant difference between Turner knowing what you needed and Turner giving you what you wanted:

"So Todd and I are good friends. So we win the Big East championship [1988–89]. So I walk into Todd's office, close the door. He's my friend. I can talk to him like I can talk to anybody. I say what I need. I need this and this and this. I need you to start treating our games like men's games, band, cheerleaders, mascot, the whole thing. We play a game, we have people running on the track. You don't do that for a men's game. Come on, close this place down, get everybody out of there, and treat it like an event. This isn't intramurals. And we're arguing, laughing back and forth, kidding. Know what the bottom line was? He said, 'No, I'm not going to do that.' And he's my friend.

"So Todd and I go have lunch. But when I got back to my office, I told Chris and the other coaches, hey, nothing is going to change here. So let's just keep getting more players, winning more games. Eventually, stuff starts to happen, but it isn't because you go in there and scream and yell. When the time comes, and it's the right time in their minds, then they will do things for you. But you're not going to make them do it until they are ready and everything else is ready."

Just a few days before Turner started on July 1, but some twenty-one years after it had first been proposed, a who's who lineup of politicians and administrators turned over symbolic shovels of earth at the official groundbreaking ceremony for the University of Connecticut Sports Center. Over the years, the complex had bobbed and weaved about the state bureaucracy without a steady hand to guide it through a black hole of red tape that included negotiating a fifty-two-step review process. Thus it was of little wonder that the projected price tag of $28.5 million was more than five times the original estimate. It was also not surprising that when completed in early 1990, it would stand as the first new athletic building on the Storrs campus since 1963, when the outdoor skating rink —which the school's hockey teams still use today—was finished.

With heavy machinery moving earth at the sports-center site and Todd Turner's new management crew plowing through the bureaucracy and institutional inertia, Calhoun closed the doors to Guyer Gym on October 15 and put his second UConn team through the 1987–88 season's first practice. It was a grueling two-hour and forty-minute workout that one of the players later described as "scary in its intensity."

Attending their first gut wrench in the gulag were six new recruits, including Lyman DePriest, Murray Williams, and Willie McCloud, who would all make immediate contributions. These additions would allow Calhoun to begin playing his pressure-defense, fast-breaking offense style. The other note of optimism at the work-ethic seminar was that Cliff Robinson and Phil Gamble had labored long and hard throughout the summer and regained their eligibility.

Although things were certainly looking up, few people were predicting anything resembling a dramatic turnabout in the team's fortunes. Even the gospel according to Calhoun was based on future salvation and realistic expectations for the here and now. "We thought about practicing at midnight," Calhoun said on the first day of official workouts, "but we think next year will be the real coming-out party."

In late November, a week before the opener with Maryland Eastern Shore, the men's basketball program took another one of those steps forward when Chris Smith of Bridgeport, one of the top point guards in the country, signed early with UConn. Not only did the acquisition of Smith further boost the goal of keeping in-state players at home, it also served notice that the days of other Big East schools waltzing into Connecticut and dancing away with such players as Charles Smith, Harold Pressley, John Pinone, and John Bagley were over. Surely, Rollie Massimino and John Thompson were no longer saying nice things about UConn's basketball coach.

Smith's mother, Lola Smith, had been very influential in her son's selection of UConn. "I trusted him," she said of Calhoun. "He seems to be an honest man. I figured anybody that interested in Chris will make sure he succeeds."

Lola Smith was not alone in her belief. Despite his 9-19 first season, the losses tying the school record, UConn fans across the state were embracing Calhoun. In crisscrossing Connecticut, tirelessly selling UConn basketball, Calhoun had sold audience after audience on the premise that the future is then but it is bright.

Meanwhile, in a less public, more meticulous, button-down, businesslike fashion, Turner was also parting the seas of neglect and sending the message that a new era was dawning. For the first time, fans were sent fancy, full-color, season-ticket applications. Corporations were contacted for support, asked to buy tickets, cosponsor advertising, promote special events. Television coverage was also increased to include games on a local station as well as a regional sports network, and Calhoun's weekly coaches' show was extended to reach throughout New England.

Yes, things were starting to jell as UConn entered the 1987–88 season, but to say that anything beyond small, personal, little moral victories was even remotely anticipated on the court would be to exaggerate expectations grossly. In a preseason story, *The Hartford Courant*'s Ken Davis defined success for the team this way: "If the Huskies can reach a competitive level where they play closer games and pull an occasional surprise, this season would be successful."

After the first nine games, which for the most part comprised the patsy portion of the team's schedule, UConn was 7-2. The record included wins over the likes of Yale, Central Connecticut, and Hartford (in double overtime) and losses to more legitimate foes such as Virginia and Villanova. At the regular season's end, UConn stood where most of the pundits figured it would be, 14-13 overall and dead last in the Big East at 4-12. As usual, UConn played in the dreaded "Black Thursday" 8-9 qualifying game of the Big East Tournament, beating Providence, but then earning an early bus ride home after losing to Pittsburgh in their opening quarterfinal game.

But there had been signs during the season that UConn might be coming on. In the conference, the team had developed a reputation for being dangerous. A 51-50 victory over Syracuse before almost thirty thousand fans at the Carrier Dome and a 66-59 triumph over Georgetown at the Hartford

Civic Center had made people take notice. Still, as a bubble team at best, there would not have been loud cries of foul if UConn's season had ended without a postseason. So when an invitation to join the thirty-two-team field for the NIT was received, surprise and a nothing-to-lose attitude greeted the news. The mere invitation was sufficient validation that the program was moving in the right direction. No one, to be sure, expected UConn to make much noise beyond grunts of effort. And then the damnedest things began to happen.

The first game was against West Virginia in Morgantown, one of the tougher places in the country for a visitor to play. Relying on defense and grit, UConn kept the Mountaineers close throughout the evening, the lead changing hands thirteen times. Then, down two, Tate George hit a running one-hander in the lane with six seconds remaining to force an overtime. In the extra session, UConn prevailed, 62-57. Back in Connecticut, where the game had been seen on a local station, on the Financial News Network of all places, fans began to stir.

Four days later, Louisiana Tech came north to play UConn at the Hartford Civic Center. Although 11,331 fans turned out for the game, attendance was still almost 5,000 short of capacity. Shooting an amazing 67.5 percent from the field, UConn won, 65-59, to advance to the quarterfinals.

Because the Hartford Civic Center was unavailable, the game against Virginia Commonwealth was played at the thirty-three-year-old Field House before a sellout-and-then-some crowd of 4,801. The scene was one Tolokan says he will never forget.

"There was never a game at UConn like that game," he

remembers. "In its own regard, it was something like the Tennessee game at Gampel Pavilion for the women's team. Talent-wise, Virginia Commonwealth was right there with us. But there was no way the crowd was going to let us lose. If you look at photographs of the game, you see this haze hanging over the floor, almost like people were smoking in there. I remember I asked Lynn McCollum, who was in charge of facilities, what it was. 'Tim,' he said, 'the crowd is making so much noise that they are shaking the dust off the rafters.' " Charged by the crowd, UConn took charge late in the second half, hitting sixteen of twenty free throws after not going to the line once in the first half, to win, 72-61.

No UConn team had ever won three games in a national postseason tournament, never mind advance to the championship, which is what UConn would do if it managed to beat Boston College in the semifinal game at Madison Square Garden. During the regular season, UConn and BC had split their Big East Conference games, each winning at home.

Boston College, riding a twenty-two-point performance by Dana Barros, led at the intermission of the rubber game by eight. If UConn were to win, Barros, who looked unstoppable, had to be contained. In the locker room at halftime, Calhoun challenged freshman Lyman DePriest to guard Barros in the second half. DePriest, one of the toughest players ever to wear a UConn uniform, responded, holding the BC star to two shots and two points. DePriest's defense and an 18-4 run sealed the victory. UConn would now meet Ohio State for a national championship.

Fans who had been slowly warming to UConn and the alien specter of success shed their New England reserve for the championship game. Governor William A. O'Neill took a helicopter to the Big Apple for the contest, followed by ten busloads of students from UConn. A Thursday night crowd of 13,779, most of them UConn fans, filled the stands by game time. Could it be possible? Could Ohio State, a national program, be defeated for a national championship by a national nobody? Most fans hoped for the best but expected the worst, winning being an acquired expectation.

In the locker room prior to taking the floor, Calhoun told the team that regardless of the outcome, he was very proud of them. It was something he had never told a team *before* a championship game.

Things did not look good for UConn early on. Robinson got into immediate foul trouble and ended up playing only twenty-three minutes, contributing only five points and two rebounds. But paced by the play of Gamble, who would score twenty-five points and be named tournament MVP, UConn led at the half, 27-25. The game was ultimately decided late in the second half, when, with the score tied at forty-six, UConn went on a 13-2 run to make it 59-48 with less than five minutes to play. In the second half, UConn hit eighteen of twenty-two from the line—after not shooting a free throw in the first half. As the final seconds ticked off the clock, Murray Williams threw the ball high into the air. UConn 72, Ohio State 67. Who would have thunk it?

Exuberant fans at Madison Square Garden stormed the court to embrace the team, while television viewers across Connecticut high-fived and four thousand students at Storrs celebrated before a huge bonfire that claimed, among other things, a Pacman machine. In the middle of the Garden party,

Calhoun watched the celebration with former coach Dee Rowe, who had been to the dance but had always left before it was over. "Here you are, James," Rowe said. "Crowds under the basket at Madison Square Garden cutting down the nets. You've won the championship. There are no more games to play."

"In all the years I have been coaching, I have never been around a group of athletes like the ones on this team," Calhoun said after the game. "We came together as a unit, and everyone understood their role."

Far from the delirium, in a small town outside New London, Dom Perno got into his car for the hour-plus drive back to his home in Bristol. Perno had called Tommy Hine, a *Hartford Courant* sportswriter who once covered UConn basketball, and asked him if he could come down and watch the game. Hine was surprised but agreed. The two grilled steaks, sipped a few beers, and watched the game. "What was funny," Hine says, "is that with about five minutes to go, Dom got up all of a sudden, said something like 'That's it,' and left. He didn't stay to watch the finish."

"I was very close to Phil, Cliff, Steve [Pikiell], Tate," Calhoun says. "I think all the fights I had were personalized in respect to these kids. I once had them crying in the locker room because I had laid such a guilt trip on them. As a result, they became a very close group. They were not a collection of all-stars, but they were pretty good and they emerged during the NIT and they started to believe. The way we played during the NIT that year, I think we would have done pretty well in the NCAA Tournament."

"What the NIT said to me was that this guy, Jim Calhoun,

can be pretty special," Tolokan says. "Look at the statistics: During the regular season, we shot maybe forty-four percent, but during the NIT we shot almost fifty-five percent. That can't happen. You just don't go from forty-four to fifty-five percent in a five-game stretch, but we did. We still didn't have great players, but Jim was able to bring them together, able to convince them for a short time that they were better than they were.

"I've always said that the NIT should never be understated because at the time it convinced people, and I think it convinced Jim Calhoun. Here he had been nine and nineteen, Cliff and Phil had flunked off the team, and he had to be wondering: Did I make the right decision? Does this place know what it takes to be successful? After winning the NIT, he started thinking: Give me a few more players, let's get the sports center finished, and I can get it done."

"I never thought that I couldn't get IT done," Calhoun says. "I just wondered what IT was. If you take the job at Kentucky, IT is a national championship. Take the job at Georgetown, and IT is a Big East and national championship. IT at Connecticut, at the time, seemed to mean, can we compete? John Toner said he'd love to be in fourth or fifth place. He was probably just being honest because that was a realistic advance from being in the eight-nine game. And people killed him for that. So the term IT became this nebulous thing that kind of floated around. The NIT showed that we could get IT done."

The championship also gave the UConn program a healthy shove in the direction of respectability in Calhoun's eyes.

"I always remember a friend of mine named Ron Green,

who took over the job at Indiana State, Larry Bird's old school. And I called him one day, and he said to me, 'Did you ever feel like you are like an ox stuck in the mud? You take a step forward, but you still keep sinking, really can't get going.' It seemed like the first years here, we knew we were making headway, we knew things were getting better, but to just get rolling here wasn't going to be good enough. You had to be able to compete with the group.

"You look at Syracuse then, Rony Seikaly, Derrick Coleman, and Sherman Douglas. Everybody was just loading up. To get things going, we needed something concrete, something definitive. And I think the NIT showed that we could go out like other teams such as Indiana had done and become a national player.

"The teams around at the end of the NIT are the same caliber teams as you will meet in the middle of the NCAA Tournament. All are good teams, all have won twenty games, all are getting better at the end of the season, all are beginning to jell. We had gone for a year and a half talking, philosophizing. We needed a notch in our belt, we needed something definitive to show, hey, we can do this. Beating Ohio State, a really good team with a national name, at Madison Square Garden became an important building block, no question. The whole package turned out perfectly for Connecticut."

Not everyone, however, was impressed. "A Top Twenty basketball program is less important than a top-twenty research program," noted one UConn professor. "If we're going to aspire to an outstanding sports program, then we ought to aspire to an outstanding academic program." Added another, "I'll get excited when the university starts winning

Nobel Prizes." Clearly, there were still fences in need of mending.

In the aftermath of the NIT, after two years of twelve-hour days, no weekends off, and nonstop work, Jim Calhoun took his first vacation since leaving Northeastern. Left behind, for the moment, was a self-created monster called expectation. After a national championship in year two, what would be the measure of success for year three?

High Expectations

To appreciate the level of expectation going into the 1988–89 season, it is important to first understand UConn basketball fans, which, not surprisingly, no one does.

Put your average UConn fan on a couch next to your average Freudian, and in less time than it takes to call for security, the courageous doctor will have discovered that he is talking to someone with more mood swings, more contradictions, more multiple personalities per square inch of tortured psyche than Sybil. As a group, UConn fans can go from loudmouth to church mouse, fun bunch to lynch mob, euphoric to the suicide hot line in the course of a single possession. And often do.

Geno Auriemma and Jim Calhoun, the two men who most often, and most intensely, feel the fans' warmth as well as their wrath, are as confused as everyone else regarding what makes the time bomb tick.

"They're schizophrenic," Auriemma says. "They want to win so bad, to be part of a winner so bad, that they don't know how to be winners. But there is no one happier when they win, but they don't appreciate winning because they are afraid they are going to lose."

Calhoun's analysis is equally fuzzy: "They are somewhat similar to Red Sox fans with a kind of Chicken-Little-the-sky-is-falling, Murphy's Law mentality," he explains. "If something good is going on, they are waiting for something bad to happen. If something bad is going on, they don't expect something good to go on. And they are always nervous. We can be up fifteen, and there is dead silence in the building because we had been up twenty. Even after all the success we have had, they are still always waiting for the hammer to drop."

Strange as it may seem, if you are from Connecticut, Auriemma's and Calhoun's descriptions make perfect sense. If you are not from Connecticut, you have a better chance of comprehending astral physics. "You have to live here to know what it is like," Calhoun says. "It is not just an affinity for the basketball team, being loyal to old State U. It is a passionate, passionate love affair that in a moment can turn to hatred— for a moment."

Just ask Dom Perno. During his last season, Perno was often booed unmercifully, and the most awful, personal things were said about him on sports talk shows and in the newspapers. But a month after his resignation, he was introduced at the annual UConn Club Dinner and received a standing ovation from many of the very same people who had screamed for his scalp.

Just how fanatical is the following for UConn basketball?

Coverage: The UConn men are followed by the largest media contingent of any college basketball team in the country. The media mob even has its own nationally known name, "The Horde." As many as fourteen daily newspapers track the team on the road, and more than twenty papers staff home games.

The UConn women have begun to attract the same level of interest from the Connecticut press corps. At the conclusion of the 1994–95 season, more than 150 media credentials were issued for NCAA Tournament games at Gampel Pavilion.

Television: The UConn men easily draw the highest local TV ratings in the Big East Conference and receive among the highest local ratings in the country. For the 1995–96 season, the UConn women will have the most extensive women's basketball local television package in the nation, period.

Radio: All UConn men's and most women's games are broadcast on the UConn Radio Network, whose flagship station is WTIC-AM, a fifty-thousand-watt powerhouse that reaches into parts of twenty-three states and Canada.

Fan support: Since the 1989–90 season, the UConn men have recorded fifty-one straight home sellouts, including twenty-four at the 16,294-seat Hartford Civic Center. Since Gampel Pavilion (8,241) opened in January of 1990, there has never been a men's game there that was not a sellout. Meanwhile, the UConn women had eight advance sellouts in 1994–95, including all of their six final games. Overall, the team averaged 7,875 fans at home, which ranks them as number three nationally.

An interesting adjunct to the increased popularity of the UConn women is that to a large extent the team is attracting support from an entirely new fan base: women, young families, junior high school girls, and senior citizens. As a result, interest in UConn basketball has been expanded to include segments of the population that had previously been unafflicted.

Tickets: Eligibility for season tickets to UConn men's games is based on a point system that centers on such things as donations, longevity, and support for other university sports. If someone were to enter the system cold, it would require a donation in excess of $8,000 just to move high enough up on the list to be able to purchase season tickets at Gampel Pavilion or the lower areas of the Hartford Civic Center. UConn women's tickets are distributed on a similar system.

Chris Dailey, who grew up in New Jersey, remembers coming away with the usual outsider's confusion following her first exposure to UConn fans: "Geno and I were out recruiting, and we went to our men's game with Syracuse at the Hartford Civic Center. The men were struggling at the time, but it was the largest crowd to ever watch a college basketball game in New England. I remember turning to Geno and saying, 'Why are these people here?' "

The short answer is because UConn fans take to a winner the way an heir takes to a rich aunt with a bad cough. Why did they turn out in record numbers to see a mediocre team play high-powered Syracuse? Quite simply because at the time

UConn had a history of upsetting the Orangemen on a regular basis.

Nowhere is a local winner embraced more ardently than in Connecticut. And this penchant for bandwagon-jacking isn't exclusive to UConn basketball. It runs the entire spectrum, success being more important than sport. Give the average Connecticut sports fan a winner and he will be out front following the charge to glory in about the time it takes to sell him the appropriate hat and T-shirt.

Exaggeration? Consider just a few examples:

UConn soccer in the early 1980s, when the team was a perennial national power and six thousand fans routinely attended games.

The Hartford Whalers in 1985–86, when the team made the Stanley Cup Playoffs and people waited hours in line to buy tickets and then honored the team with a parade after it was eliminated in the division finals.

And then there is UConn baseball in the spring of 1990, when the team qualified for the NCAA Tournament. During the regular season, fifty to seventy-five fans attended games. But then the team got hot for the Big East Tournament and walked away with the conference's automatic bid. In the first round, they were scheduled to meet Georgia at Municipal Stadium in Waterbury. Some eight thousand fans turned out for the game—so many fans, in fact, that totally unprepared NCAA officials had to let people in free because they did not have enough ticket takers, and backed-up fans were blocking the street outside.

The reason Connecticut fans are shameless front-runners is rooted in an inferiority complex fostered and fueled by the state's location midway between East Coast egocentrics Boston and New York City. Bostonians consider conservative, insurance-industry-dominated Connecticut the filing cabinet of New England. To New Yorkers, the state is little more than a suburb. These superior attitudes, coupled with the fact that Connecticut does not have the wide array of professional and college rooting options its supercilious neighbors have, causes a state of mass hysteria to spread whenever a local standard-bearer receives acclaim. The fact that UConn's basketball teams have, of late, routinely beaten the snot out of St. John's and Boston College also provides no small measure of satisfaction.

While UConn men's basketball certainly gains additional interest when things are going well, it is important to note that the program has traditionally had a large and loyal fan base. "There has always been a lot of interest in basketball here," Calhoun says. "I don't have to create interest. I was very cognizant of that when I came here."

To trace the history of UConn basketball is to find a bloodline of fan support dating back to the very first game, on February 8, 1901. The Connecticut Agricultural College Aggies defeated Willimantic High School, 17-12, in that historic contest. Students chartered a mule-driven sleigh for the inaugural road trip, which, according to the school newspaper, proved to be a huge success. "With fine sleighing on a fine night, Mr. Knowles [the team captain] took our team to Willimantic and to the honor of our team it may be said that the students, the young ladies especially, took enough interest in the boys in the blue and white jerseys to cheer lustily during the entire game."

Being a fan in the beginning often called for complete commitment. One of the game's early rules mandated that the first player to touch the ball after it went out of bounds was awarded possession. (Makes one wonder how sought after front-row seats at Gampel Pavilion would be today if such a rule still existed.)

The first games were played in College Hall, which was located in Old Main, the primary building on campus. The room not only served as basketball court but also dance hall and chapel. It wasn't until 1914–15 that the Aggies played in their first basketball facility, Hawley Armory.

In 1929–30, a Connecticut basketball team got a taste of fan-induced pressure when it played Yale for the first time. The crowd in New Haven was so large, and so boisterous, that the jittery Aggies had only four points in the first half.

Preseason expectations were experienced prior to the 1938–39 season, when a team comprised of promising sophomores was expected to meld with a solid nucleus of veterans. The team was initially dubbed "The Wonder Team," but after losing six of its first nine games, fans had a new name for the squad: "Flash in the Pan."

In 1946–47, UConn went 16-2 and tickets to games in Hawley Armory were in such demand that an alternating-game policy was instituted, meaning fans were only able to see four of the eight home games.

The 1950s served as the breeding ground for what is now known as "Huskymania," and established the insatiable appetite for success that gnaws at and graces UConn basketball today. During the ten seasons between 1949–50 and 1958–59, UConn compiled a record of 186-68 under coach Hugh

Greer, went to the NCAA Tournament six times, and won the Yankee Conference nine times. The team became so popular that "The Cage," the new 3,400-seat on-campus basketball facility, was inadequate as soon as it was finished. And when the 4,500-seat Field House opened in 1954–55, it was too small from the moment the doors were unlocked.

Commenting on the team's popularity and the difficulty in obtaining tickets to games, *Hartford Courant* columnist Frank Keys in 1956 offered what was then considered a far-out solution in his column: "The only way I can think of to overcome the seating problem, which is acute now and will worsen in the near future, will be television. That's not as ridiculous as it reads. . . . If anyone can think of another answer to the UConn problem besides television, send your ideas to Storrs. No one among the university wheels would care to ask the legislature for money to build a new and larger basketball arena when the present one is still in its infancy. But the sports-minded citizens of our land of steady habits want to see the Huskies play. They have to be satisfied one way or the other."

Continued success kept the hunger for UConn basketball ravenous through the mid-1960s. Players such as Toby Kimball and Wes Bialosuknia were revered throughout the state, and fans braved New England winters to watch them play at home and on the road. After Greer died unexpectedly of a heart attack in 1963, his successor, Fred Shabel, took over, compiling a 72-29 record in four seasons and going to the NCAA Tournament three times.

Although such sustained success would not come again for almost twenty years, the double-edged sword called "Huskymania" had been forged. Now, as the 1988–89 season approached, it was unsheathed once again and honed to a razor's edge by anticipation. Certainly there was cause for optimism. All five starters and seven of the first eight players, including the highest single-season scoring duo in UConn history, Cliff Robinson and Phil Gamble, were returning from the NIT championship team. But basketball is played on wood, not paper, which would become all too apparent as the season played out.

UConn began the season of high hopes as it had left off the year before, winning. Included in the opening 9-1 run was a 68-61 road victory over the University of Virginia in the fifth game and a two-point triumph over Villanova. The only setback during the early going was a fifteen-point loss to Purdue. Following the quick start, reality in the form of the Big East portion of the schedule kicked in, and the team went 7-10 during the remainder of the regular season. Among the defeats were some tough losses: 80-78 to Providence, 68-62 to Syracuse, 59-55 to Georgetown, and 72-69 to Seton Hall.

In the Big East, UConn finished tied for seventh with a 6-10 record and was defeated in the opening round of the conference tournament. A second straight invitation to the NIT was accepted, and in the tournament UConn won its first two games before falling to Alabama-Birmingham in the quarterfinals.

"For me personally, 1988–89 was the hardest year, because I knew we had made progress," Calhoun says. "We weren't just a gnat anymore. We started to get real close to folks. And we had some real, real tough games where we just didn't get over the top. But progress had been made. We knew we could do it. And to be honest, I was a little taken aback by people saying, well, he's good enough to get us going but he really can't get it."

During the season, Calhoun was not disappointed with the way the team was playing, but he admitted afterward to being a bit discouraged because of the negative reaction. The problem, of course, was the unrealistic expectations stemming from the NIT championship.

"Sure, we won the NIT and beat Ohio State," Calhoun says, "but we only won six games in the Big East that year and lost ten. We weren't a five hundred team yet. It was going to take time to build a program. That's why I had a seven-year contract.

"There seemed to be a lot of, not hostility, but frustration. People blamed Cliff Robinson. Yet he averaged twenty points and ten rebounds, and we haven't had anybody do that since. Cliff was not a great college player. He was a great talent, a kid who you could see was evolving. Cliff didn't know if he wanted to be Darth Vader or Bambi. But Cliff and Phil Gamble helped set up the era.

"In retrospect, you had to go through one of those seasons where you were close, but not close enough. Then the choice became building on that, or being discouraged by it."

The Israeli Connection

He came out of the Middle East wrapped in intrigue.

From nowhere he was suddenly everywhere in the fall of 1989, walking the Storrs campus, playing pickup games with the team, running the cemetery hill. Who was this stranger, this unheralded arrival whose name suggested a code word, whose murky background included military training. Who was this man called "The Dove"?

Certainly he was not your average UConn basketball recruit. The very fact that little was known about him made him different. As a matter of course, the usual UConn recruit is as well known as the governor by the time he arrives. The player's high school accomplishments are common knowledge, as are his stats, strengths and weaknesses, blue-chip status, SAT scores, height and weight, favorite foods, turn-ons and turnoffs.

But Nadav Henefeld was unlike any other player ever to wear a UConn uniform. He was not from such hoop hotbeds as Washington, New York, or L.A. In fact, he wasn't even from this country. He was from Israel, of all places, a country renowned for many things, basketball definitely *not* being one of them.

In the long term, this tall, dark, and heads-up Israeli with the understated game would become one of the most important recruits in UConn history. He would be the player to open a pipeline that would come to be known as "The Israeli Connection." Although Henefeld would remain for only one season, his play and his popularity would solidify a relationship that would yield three more Israeli players. One, Doron Sheffer, may be good enough to be drafted by an NBA team in the first round.

While Calhoun is now careful to maintain and nurture the association, visiting Israel each year to conduct clinics and speak, the marriage was more accidental than arranged. Calhoun was in Yugoslavia in the summer of 1987 and on the way home stopped in Tel Aviv to give an additional clinic. His work impressed some people, and before he left he asked that they remember him if they ever came across a good player who wanted to play in the USA. The contact was the type coaches make all the time, routine, no big deal. And Calhoun quickly forgot about it.

In April of 1989, however, Calhoun got a call from Marv Kessler, a former coach at Adelphi who had also done some coaching in Israel. "Marv told me that there was a kid down at St. John's who he had coached in Israel. He said the kid didn't like St. John's and he didn't think he liked Carnesecca, but he loved basketball: 'What he is looking for is a college campus. Why don't you have him up, he's only going to be here a few more days.' "

On the day Henefeld was scheduled to return to Israel on a 9 P.M. flight, UConn assistant coach Dave Leitao drove to New York City, picked him up at 5:30 A.M., and brought him to Storrs. Henefeld's visit lasted only five hours, but it was long enough for him to fall in love with the campus and the rural environment.

Calhoun, however, was not about to give a scholarship to a kid from Israel he had never seen play. So he put Henefeld off for the moment. In July, Calhoun flew to Tel Aviv for the Maccabiah Games. After watching Henefeld play several times during his five-day visit and be named MVP, Calhoun offered him a scholarship. "I was very, very impressed," Calhoun says.

But there were still obstacles to overcome. To attain academic eligibility, Henefeld had to score 700 on the SATs. In April he had taken the test but fallen forty points short. As a high school student in Israel, Henefeld had received high grades, but differences in language, culture, and an understanding of the nature of the test combined to cause him problems. In September, he was given permission to take the test again. In order to receive the results quickly, Henefeld flew to Raleigh, North Carolina, in mid-October at his own expense to take the test a second time. This time he scored over 800. Academically, all he had to do now was earn passing grades in a very unfreshmanlike course load that included chemistry, geology, English, and Hebrew.

Just when it seemed everything was in place, another potential problem cropped up, this one smacking of international sabotage. The NCAA received a letter postmarked Paris, written in Hebrew, claiming that Henefeld should be ineligible to play college basketball because he had been paid for playing some games in Israel. Following investigations by the NCAA and the University of Connecticut, the allegations were found to be false and Henefeld was cleared to play. Who was behind the letter and why remains an unsolved mystery. Lou Carnesecca is not believed to read and write Hebrew.

By the time practice began in mid-October, Henefeld was feeling more and more comfortable in his new country, one much different from his own. Henefeld grew up in Ramat Ha Sharon, which is located about fifteen minutes outside Tel Aviv. His mother died when he was six, and he was raised by his father, Zeev, and his sister, Anat, who is four years older. Zeev Henefeld, an engineer who runs a small metals factory, stands six-foot-three and played a little basketball in his youth.

Nadav, who was tall for his age, began playing when he was nine and picked up the game quickly. He honed his skills at the local athletic club as opposed to the driveway or playground, the organized leagues and instruction contributing much to the sound fundamental style that is the cornerstone of his game.

Following his graduation from high school, Henefeld entered the military to serve his mandatory three years of active duty. Everyone in Israel, men and women, must serve in the military and then remain on reserve status until age fifty-five. Because of his basketball prowess, Henefeld's main job following basic training was playing and practicing with the Is-

raeli National Team, where he gained a reputation as one of
the country's best players.

While in the military, Henefeld wrote letters and sent his
statistics to about twenty U.S. colleges, getting polite re-
sponses but little interest. St. John's was one of the few that
even considered taking a look. At about the same time,
Henefeld was challenging the Israeli club basketball system in
court. Israeli players' assignment to clubs is determined by
where they grew up. Henefeld did not want to play for the
club that held his rights, but the courts upheld the system.

In truth, if St. John's had had dorms, he probably would
have gone there. But in Storrs, he found the living arrangements he wanted, the campus atmosphere he preferred, and a
coaching staff he liked.

"He was really quiet when he first got here," Tate George
recalls. "We'd be playing pickup games and he'd just sit on
the sidelines until someone would say, 'Hey, Dove, you want
to play?' Then he'd say Okay and walk out onto the court.
But he earned our respect right after the first game."

While Henefeld did not have the usual attributes found in
American players—size, quickness, or leaping ability—he had
other assets. He was a good shooter, excellent passer, and
strong positional rebounder. He could also run and was the
third fastest player on the team over thirty yards, finishing
ahead of such athletic teammates as Scott Burrell, Chris
Smith, and John Gwynn. But perhaps his greatest gift was
instinct, knowing where everyone was on the court at all
times and always being a half step ahead of the action. "His
understanding of the game is intuitive," Calhoun says.

Henefeld's sense of anticipation was particularly evident on

defense. He set the UConn single-season record for steals
(138) on a team that averaged more than thirteen steals per
game, which is an NCAA Division I record. So adept was
Henefeld at swiping the ball that one New York tabloid
dubbed him "The Gaza Stripper."

Initially, Henefeld had to adjust to the size and quickness of
the American players and the speed at which the game is
played. But it didn't take long for him to input the data and
output the information on court. Soon his teammates were
calling him "Little Bird," which had nothing to do with
doves and everything to do with Larry and the way Henefeld
resembled the Celtics superstar when snapping one of his perfect look-away passes.

There was also the matter of Calhoun to be gotten used to.
Henefeld had never experienced practices of such intensity, of
such seriousness. And he had never had a coach so willing to
get into a player's face, slap him upside the psyche, and stomp
around on his ego. At first, Calhoun was reluctant to press
Henefeld because of his unique situation. But as the Israeli
became more comfortable, Calhoun became more inclined to
treat him like everyone else. Henefeld welcomed the abuse.
He didn't want to be treated any differently than anyone else.
He wanted to be just one of the guys. He wanted to be
treated like a basketball player.

But there were more than just the usual freshman pressures
on the soft-spoken Israeli. There was also pressure from
home, pressure to represent his country in international competition. Early in the season, bowing to that pressure,
Henefeld flew to Tel Aviv on November 18 to play in a game
against France. On November 22, he scored twenty-three

points in that game, leading Israel to a 99-93 victory. Two hours later he was on a plane bound for the Great Alaska Shootout via New York, Seattle, and Anchorage. The trip took twenty-six hours, twenty of which were in the air. At the Shootout, Henefeld had twenty-nine points, fifteen rebounds, five assists, and a team-high thirteen steals in three games.

Just as Henefeld had snuck up on Calhoun and his staff, he also surprised UConn basketball fans. He did not start at first, but after ten games, when Burrell went down with a knee injury, he got the nod during the Connecticut Mutual Classic. Henefeld was promptly named the MVP, and the faithful were in love. Although UConn fans embrace a fast-paced, up-and-down, slam-and-jam style, they also possess a keen understanding of the game. They have an eye for, and an appreciation of, basketball's nuances: the weak-side pick, the creative pass, the steal that is all anticipation. In Henefeld, they found another dimension of the game, one based more on fundamentals than flash, in intellect more than physical ability, in subtlety more than spectacle.

By mid-January, Henefeld was the most popular player on a most popular team. Everyone wanted to know about him. Everyone wanted to meet him, to talk to him, to be him. Kids in the driveway were suddenly Nadav Henefeld taking the last shot at the buzzer. Nonnewaug High School had eight steals in the fourth quarter to win a game, and afterward the players were chanting "Nadav, Nadav, Nadav" in the locker room.

Homemade signs such as "Welcome to the Dove Dome" were flashed at every game. Somewhere in the stands, a large Israeli flag was usually being waved from side to side. And when Henefeld was voted Big East Player of the Week, the first freshman to win the award, he received one of those rafters-dust-loosening ovations as he walked to center court to accept the plaque.

In the Jewish community, interest in Henefeld was extremely high. The weekly *Connecticut Jewish Ledger* began staffing games, and the New York bureaus of large Israeli newspapers routinely requested results. Sid Frankel, a butcher and college basketball junkie from Waterbury, collected every story written on Henefeld and sent them to a paper in Tel Aviv. *Ma'ariv,* the second largest paper in Tel Aviv, sent a writer to cover the Big East Tournament, while *Yedioth Ahronot,* the largest paper, did a huge spread.

Israeli sports pages were filled with Henefeld's exploits on the court and the impact he was having off it. Never had an Israeli basketball player done so well and been so recognized. "Whenever a Jew rises athletically, everyone in the Jewish Community takes great pride," Phil Jacobs, editor of the internationally circulated *Jewish Times* of Baltimore, noted. "Jews have been typecast as not being great athletes. Usually we are seen as the guy who owns the team or manages it. Now we have this soldier from Israel who comes to the United States and excels at our game. People are very turned on by this."

Nor was Henefeld neglected by Connecticut's Jewish mothers. He received more invitations to spend the holidays than the local rabbi. On one occasion, a mother approached the reserved Henefeld with her mortified daughter in tow. "Here, take my daughter," she said to Henefeld. "And if you don't want her, take me." Suffice it to say, teammates who witnessed the scene did not let Henefeld soon forget it.

"People like Doron Sheffer a great deal," Calhoun says, "but they *loved* Nadav. He was handsome, charismatic, and he had a way about him."

Henefeld finished his freshman season by being named Big East Rookie of the Year, Big East Rookie of the Week three times, and Big East Player of the Week once. He averaged 11.6 points on 48 percent shooting and 38 percent from three-point land while finishing second in the nation with a school-record 138 steals.

And then he was gone. Without warning he vanished back into the Middle East in August of 1990. The move came without any prior indications. He had gone back to Israel after the season but then returned to Storrs. He had even worked as a counselor at Red Auerbach's basketball camp. But on August 10, Calhoun got an overseas call from Henefeld, who told him he had decided to turn professional in Israel and was signing a contract the next day. Pressure to return home and play in the Israeli National League and for the Israeli National Team was reported to be the reason. Fans were shocked and saddened when they heard the news, but there was no animosity, no sense of betrayal. The Dove had given them too much.

"His leaving after one season made him an even bigger hero, made him bigger than life," Calhoun says. "Here is this mysterious man who all of a sudden appears one morning with the sunrise and then rides out with the sunset after having done great and wonderful deeds. Nadav is without doubt the most romantic thing I have ever seen in college basketball, in sports."

Calhoun also says Henefeld was the key in establishing

UConn's relationship with Israel. And that relationship, Calhoun maintains, has helped establish a recruiting base in other European countries.

Today, Henefeld plays for Maccabi–Tel Aviv in the Israeli Club League, where he continues to wow fans with his pleasing style. He is also an international star with the Israeli National Team. While at UConn, Henefeld used to send tapes of games back home to family and friends. "These let people see the games," he said at the time, "but they don't let people see the excitement."

(Because of Henefeld, and now Sheffer, UConn basketball has become very popular in Israel, with a dozen or so games shown on television throughout the country each season.)

Although Henefeld was gone, the connection was continued in the 1990–91 season with the arrival of another Israeli National Team member, Gilad Katz, a six-foot-three guard from Tel Aviv. Katz would make a contribution to the UConn program over the next two years but in a reserve role. In 1994, Uri Cohen-Mintz, a member of the Israeli undertwenty-two national team, would also play for UConn, but he, too, would see only limited time.

The UConn women also benefited from the relationship with Israel when Orly Grossman, a member of the Israeli National Team, signed on for the 1990–91 season. Grossman, a guard/forward, was endorsed by Henefeld, who compared her play to that of Kris Lamb. "I think she came to Connecticut because of all the attention Nadav was getting in Israel," Dailey says.

Grossman committed to UConn for two years, but left after one year when the Gulf War broke out. "It was difficult for her," Dailey says. "I remember we played Syracuse and after the game we had to tell her that a bomb had hit in Tel Aviv.

"With foreign kids it's always difficult because you don't know how long they are going to stay. And the language barrier can be a problem. But Orly was terrific. She got along well with the kids and spoke good English. It was funny because she would take notes half in English and half in Hebrew. She was an excellent student in physical therapy. She still calls once in a while."

In between Katz and Cohen-Mintz, the third Israeli player in five years, Doron Sheffer, joined the UConn program in 1993. Unlike Henefeld, Sheffer was a much-sought-after recruit. His trip to the United States in search of a college was a whirlwind seven-day excursion in which he visited Kentucky, Miami, Seton Hall, and Temple as well as UConn. He settled on UConn because he felt comfortable with the educational opportunities as well as the basketball situation.

Comparisons to Henefeld were naturally forthcoming, but Sheffer had already dealt with that in Israel. Playing for Galil Elyon in the Israeli Club League, Sheffer led his team to the national championship in 1992–93, averaging 13.6 points and 5.8 assists per game and being named league MVP. The previous year, he had scored forty points against Henefeld and Maccabi–Tel Aviv in a game during the national semifinals. While Calhoun calls both Henefeld and Sheffer great players, he thinks Sheffer may be the better of the two. He is certainly the better shooter.

In two years at UConn, Sheffer has averaged 11.5 points while starting sixty-six of sixty-seven games and playing almost thirty minutes per game. He was Big East Rookie of the

Year in 1993–94 and second team All Big East in 1994–95, the same year he was named UConn Scholar Athlete.

Although Sheffer has not captured fans in the emotional way Henefeld did, he is nonetheless a crowd favorite for many of the same reasons: the unflappable demeanor—his nickname is "The Israeli Iceman"—and the same sound fundamental game.

Following his second season, there was concern that Sheffer would move on, perhaps return home or make himself available for the NBA draft. But in May of 1995, he issued a statement that sent an audible whew throughout Connecticut: "After much thought about my future, it is now clear to me that the decision which allows me to feel the best about myself is to return to UConn for my final season of college basketball and to try and do as much as I can to fulfill my goal and my dream of playing professional basketball in the National Basketball Association."

In Sheffer's first two years at UConn, the team has compiled a record of 57-10, won the Big East title twice, and advanced to the Sweet Sixteen and Final Eight of the NCAA Tournament. "If you take the three years when we had Henefeld or Sheffer, our records were thirty-one, twenty-nine, and twenty-eight victories," Calhoun says. "I don't think anyone will argue that that's been a pretty good connection."

The Dream Season

In the winter of 1989–90, Connecticut was a state of hysteria. The condition was caused by exposure to an affliction known as Huskus Roundballus Fanaticus, or Huskymania. The fever had existed to varying degrees within the confines of Connecticut for almost ninety years. But never had the outbreak been as widespread or as virulent. So severe, so contagious, so debilitating, so delusional was the episode that it became known simply as "The Dream Season."

Just as even the greatest plague begins with a single flea, so too did the Dream Season have a humble start. Surely, when the team officially assembled for the first time, no one was predicting a Big East championship, a Final Eight appearance in the NCAA Tournament, or a 31-6 record. Nor could any-one predict the obsession the team would become locally, or that it would be adopted by the nation as the season's Cinderella story, or that a single shot during the team's journey would be heard around the basketball world. And certainly no one could have foreseen that after the season had played itself to a nail-chomping conclusion, UConn men's basketball would begin measuring itself against the top programs in the country.

Question marks, as opposed to expectations, greeted the players assembling on October 15. The high hopes following the NIT championship had been dashed upon reality's rocky shores, leaving everyone more cautious about sailing heart-first into uncharted waters. The known commodities could be counted on one hand: Tate George, Lyman DePriest, Murray Williams, and Steve Pikiell, though he too was iffy because of a chronically bad shoulder. The rest of the team was divided between those who could be labeled either as who knows or wait and sees. Consider their ranks:

Nadav Henefeld, whom no one had ever seen play.

Chris Smith, who had struggled somewhat his freshman year.

Scott Burrell, a gifted athlete, but a freshman.

Rod Sellers, an undersized center.

John Gwynn, a streaky shooter.

Dan Cyrulik, seven-foot-one but passive.

Toraino Walker, a fierce rebounder, but also a freshman.

Calhoun was also cautious about the team's prospects. But early on he had gotten a sense of the commitment the players were making as a group. He also liked his overall personnel.

"There were a lot of questions to be answered coming in," Calhoun says, "but there were also a lot of answers. I knew Chris Smith was going to be good. Tate George felt he had something to prove. We knew Scott Burrell was a great athlete, but we didn't realize how mature a competitor he was. Rod Sellers was continuing to improve dramatically, and then there were the other pieces, Murray Williams, Toraino Walker, Lyman DePriest, Dan Cyrulik. The key was probably Nadav. He was far and away so much better than we had expected. He brought us two or three players in one. He was mature. He was very stoic. And he always expected to win. He was just this incredible ingredient that was terrific for the team."

Based on the potential of his assembled talent, Calhoun had decided to take a calculated risk during the summer. Although he felt the program had been established during his first three years, he hadn't yet opened up the team's style of play. Now he felt he had the people to take that chance. He knew it could mean getting buried at times, which happened, but Calhoun believed he now had enough offensive weapons to make a war of it.

"The other thing that I think helped us was the lack of expectation," Calhoun says. "People weren't sure about us. The eighteen wins coming off the NIT championship had thrown them off-kilter. They had expected more. Going into this season, I don't think anyone was going to overreact if we weren't as good."

In the preseason poll of Big East coaches, UConn was picked to finish eighth in the nine-team conference. And in the team's first game in the Great Alaska Shootout, they were stunned, 92-81, by Texas A&M, a football school. UConn recovered from the loss, beating Auburn and then Florida State before heading back to the lower forty-eight. Five more victories followed to bring the team's record to 7-1. Although the numbers looked good, several of the victories were against such teams as Yale, Hartford, and Maine. The ninth game of the season, against Villanova at the Hartford Civic Center, was one Calhoun says he has never forgotten. "It was the last time we were booed," Calhoun says of the 64-57 loss. "We have never been booed at home since then."

After taking out the Villanova defeat on Southern Connecticut, 100-37, and breezing through the Connecticut Mutual Classic, UConn ventured again into the Big East, meeting St. John's in New York City. The game reinforced Calhoun's worst fears when he had decided to open up the offense. St. John's simply took names, 93-62. UConn was now 10-3 overall and 0-2 in the Big East. But the worst was over, and the good times were about to roll.

In short order, UConn defeated Pittsburgh, Villanova, Seton Hall, and Syracuse. The next opponent was Georgetown, and the matchup was the latest biggest game in school history. The Hoyas were ranked number two at the time and were undefeated at 14-0. A victory would assure them of becoming the number one team in the country. Cheered on by a raucous Hartford Civic Center crowd, UConn jumped out to a 14-0 lead, then fought and scratched its way to a 70-65 win.

Henefeld and the Steel Curtain Defense were the stars of the game. The calm and confident Israeli had twenty-one points, including five three-pointers, to go along with five rebounds, five assists, and five steals. For the first time in school history, UConn had won five straight games in the Big East. "It's the biggest win since I have been here at Connecticut," Calhoun said after the game. "We're a good basketball team that's developing into a *very* good basketball team."

Looking back, Calhoun says: "The team didn't have the offensive talent of some of the kids we have had in the past couple of years, but it had a toughness to it. And, as it turned out, was the best pressing team in the history of college basketball. It averaged more steals per game than any team ever has. We found a suitable style to suit the team. Everyone on the team could run, it wasn't fast-break-oriented, it was pressing. The parts all just seemed to fit. And we had taken the chance of opening the floor up. People couldn't believe Georgetown could be down fourteen and O. In the NCAA Tournament, California had twenty turnovers in the first half. It was just a unique team with unique individuals."

Former UCLA coach John Wooden said UConn's press reminded him of his own 1963–64 team, which he said had the best press he had ever seen. Gail Goodrich, a standout on Wooden's teams, told Calhoun he taped Connecticut's games just to study the press.

On the evening of January 27, UConn was scheduled to open its decades-in-the-planning sports complex, the Harry A. Gampel Pavilion. With the addition of Gampel, UConn would play its home games on three different home courts during the season. The breakdown included five at Gampel, five at the Field House, and eight at the Hartford Civic Center. Although the table location may have changed, the home cooking proved to be consistent. As things would ultimately play out, UConn would lose only one home game the entire season, the 64-57 loss to Villanova in early December that Calhoun refuses to forget.

As if it had been scripted, the opponent for the Gampel opener was St. John's, who had humbled UConn earlier in the season and was now ranked number fifteen. The game was close in the first half, UConn getting a nice halftime lift when Chris Smith hit a three-pointer at the buzzer for a 35-34 edge. In the second half, Gwynn and Cyrulik scored twenty of UConn's first twenty-five points, and, spurred by the crowd, UConn went on to win 72-58, a forty-five-point turnaround from their previous meeting. It was also the team's seventh straight Big East Conference win and moved them into a first-place tie at 6-2.

Over the next ten games, UConn would go 8-2 (6-2 in the Big East) to finish the regular season with a 12-4 conference mark, 25-5 overall. The conference record was good enough for a share of the Big East regular-season title with Syracuse, and it also marked the biggest one-season turnaround in conference history, from seventh in 1988–89 to first. And this was accomplished by a team that had been picked to finish eighth. "It brought tears to my eyes when I thought how far this program had come," said Tate George, who recalled, all too vividly, the bad old days.

Five days after the end of the regular season, UConn traveled to New York City and the Big East Tournament at Madison Square Garden. The goal was no secret. Win the whole damn thing and grab the automatic berth to the NCAA Tournament.

The first game was against Seton Hall, and the game plan was simple: Press for forty minutes. Although UConn shot only 41.5 percent, they limited Seton Hall to 36.5 percent

The Husky Dog holding the new mascot.

Jim Calhoun—hard work and intensity.

John Gwynn celebrates big-time.

Tate George after missing the steal of a pass that would have beaten Duke
and sent UConn to the Final Four in the Dream Season.

Nadav Henefeld started the Israeli Connection.

Always number one in the hearts of Husky fans.

A towering Donyell Marshall.

Scott Burrell rebounds, Henefeld in back.

Earl Kelley elevates his game.

THE HARTFORD COURANT

Chris Smith was pivotal in state recruit.

UCONN ATHLETIC DEPT.

Cliff Robinson—
Darth Vader or Bambi?

Huskymania has many faces.

Geno Auriemma is carried off the floor after winning
the National Championship.

Coach Auriemma on the phone with President Clinton
after the championship game.

Fans greeting the victorious UConn women at the airport.

The reception at the Gampel Pavilion.

Pam Webber (left) and Rebecca Lobo.

Jen Rizzotti,
driven to excel.

Kerry Bascom displays All-American
form.

Wendy Davis—
nobody shot it better.

Chris Dailey, Meghan Pattyson, and Wendy Davis were all key recruits.

Rebecca Lobo lets the world know who's number one.

from the field. They also stole the ball seventeen times, resulting in twenty-four Seton Hall turnovers. Final score, 76-58.

The next opponent was number five Georgetown, with
whom number eight UConn had split during the regular season. It was UConn's first visit to the semifinals since 1980.
Georgetown had a 36-30 lead at halftime and led 47-39 with
just over thirteen minutes remaining. But then UConn went
on a 14-0 run, holding Georgetown scoreless for over eight
minutes. Georgetown fought back to make the score 53-52 in
the closing minutes, but then UConn hit eight straight free
throws to clinch the victory, 65-60. What made it even more
impressive was that it was done without Rod Sellers, who had
been lost in the first two minutes of the game with a knee
injury.

The conference championship game came down to the two
regular-season Big East title holders, UConn and number
four Syracuse. Again, UConn and Syracuse had split during
the regular season, each winning at home. UConn would be
without the services of Sellers, who played only two minutes,
while Syracuse would be led by their All-American center,
Derrick Coleman.

Syracuse started quickly, scoring the first ten points, but
then, midway through the half, UConn went on one of its
patented 12-0 runs to cut the margin and take a 42-35 advantage into the locker room at halftime. This was not an insig-
nificant development in that UConn was 26-0 on the season
when leading at the half.

Ahead 67-65 with four minutes to go, UConn would not
score another field goal the rest of the game. But it would hit
eleven of fourteen free throws, including six by Tate George

in the final thirty seconds, to ice the game. In winning, defense had forced twenty turnovers, while the front line had held Coleman to just five field-goal attempts in thirty-eight minutes. Final score, 78-75.

At the game's end, fans rushed onto the floor at the Garden. For the second time in two years, they were celebrating a championship in New York City. In Connecticut, a record television audience heard CBS's Brent Musburger say, "And Connecticut will win the Big East championship . . . let the celebration begin." And it did.

"I've never cut down a net before, and I didn't really want to today," Calhoun said. "But when Toraino said he would lift me up, I said, 'Yes, sir.' "

But for all the headiness and high fives, Tolokan says he thinks the accomplishment of winning the Big East Tournament was lost somewhat in the anticipation of the NCAA Tournament and the thirst for even more success.

"Just think about it," Tim Tolokan says. "In fifty-four hours, we beat Seton Hall, Georgetown, and Syracuse. But because there was such a short turnaround between us winning the Big East and then being named the top seed in the Eastern Regional of the NCAA and playing in Hartford, I always felt people never had a chance to fully appreciate what had happened in New York. So many side issues started occurring, Mike Jarvis and BU and who else was coming to Hartford. On the Monday morning we were trying to celebrate our first Big East championship, the top stories in the paper were about playing BU on Thursday and fifteen hundred tickets being available."

If luck is the residue of effort and ability, what is the root of fate, timing, destiny? While the answer to the question might not have seemed important as UConn entered the NCAA Tournament as the number one seed in the East, there was no doubt that this was a team being guided by some cosmic force.

One had to look no farther than the location for UConn's first two games to see some grand plan was at play. Years earlier, when the thought of UConn being the top seed in the East was not even a consideration, the Hartford Civic Center was selected as one of the regional's two sites for first- and second-round games. And now, here was UConn, a legitimate contender for the first time at exactly the right time playing what amounted to a home game in a national tournament. Coincidence?

Going into the first game with Boston University, the sixteenth-seed, number-three-ranked (28-5) UConn appeared to be a heavy favorite. But BU gave UConn all it could handle in the first half, and only one point separated the teams at the intermission. Four minutes into the second half, BU held a 41-38 lead. But then the UConn pressure and superior depth finally got to the Bostonians. UConn went on a 21-1 run to put the game out of reach and won 76-52.

UConn moved on to face California, which had beaten Indiana by two points and sent lovable Bobby Knight into one of his periodic press-conference tirades. Given the way the team had played against BU earlier, no one really knew what to expect when they threw the ball up. But this time UConn seemed to have its focus, and the game was essentially over in the first four minutes. UConn jumped out to a 17-2 lead and never led by less than twelve the remainder of the game, winning 74-54. Again, pressure was the difference, with UConn recording sixteen steals and forcing twenty-eight turnovers that directly resulted in twenty-five points.

With an engraved invitation to the Sweet Sixteen, UConn headed to the Meadowlands Arena in East Rutherford, New Jersey, and a meeting with Atlantic Coast Conference regular-season champion Clemson. If there was any doubt that UConn was a team of destiny, it would soon be resolved in this game by way of a single pass, a single flick of the wrist, a single tick of the clock.

The game began well for UConn, the pressure defense forcing sixteen turnovers in the opening twenty minutes, resulting in a 38-29 lead at the half. UConn continued to dominate in the second half, increasing its lead to nineteen points with little more than twelve minutes remaining. But then the intensity began to run dry, and Clemson started to claw its way back into the game. With twelve seconds to go, Clemson hit a three-pointer to take the lead, 70-69.

Following a time-out, UConn came up the floor and worked the ball. George missed a relatively uncontested fourteen-footer with time running out. UConn fouled immediately, stopping the clock with 1.6 seconds remaining. Clemson's Sean Tyson then proceeded to miss the front end of a one and one. UConn got the ball back and called for time with exactly one second to go in the season. The crowd was silent as the UConn players, their body language screaming defeat, headed to the sidelines. "When we came to the bench, the only guy that thought we could win was Coach," George says.

"When we lost to Florida a few years ago in the tournament, when Donyell Marshall missed the foul shots, I was very nervous about those shots," Calhoun says. "I don't know if it is good or bad, but I am somewhat that way. When I got into the huddle against Clemson, I just felt we were going to hit the shot, that we had come too far to lose. We had two plays, home run one and home run two. To run those plays and hit the shot without anyone guarding you is tough. To do it with somebody guarding you takes, well, it takes a great deal of good fortune, or fate. I'm not sure which one. It was probably hard work and opportunity and fate all meeting each other."

Scott Burrell, who had a ninety-miles-per-hour fastball and had been signed by the Toronto Blue Jays, was handed the ball when the whistle blew. He promptly threw an eighty-foot pass to George, who caught it, turned, and lofted a jump shot that passed through the net as the buzzer sounded and the college basketball world went mad. The play immediately became one of the greatest finishes in NCAA Tournament history. In UConn lore, it would thereafter be identified as "The Shot."

"The college game is not thirty-nine minutes and fifty-nine seconds long," Calhoun reminded reporters afterward. "It is forty minutes long."

Next up was the Elite Eight and a meeting with Duke. Duke had been to the Final Four the previous two years, but now it would be seeing a team that seemed to be preordained to keep on playing until there were no more games left to be contested.

Duke led by seven at the half, but UConn came back to tie it at the end of regulation on a three-pointer by Chris Smith.

In the overtime, the lead changed hands five times. Then with UConn leading by one and Duke trying to work the ball for the winning shot, George stepped in front of a Bobby Hurley pass and looked to have the steal that would give UConn the victory. But fate, being a fickle foe as well as an ally, did not look the ball into George's hands. It hit his outstretched fingers and fell to the floor, out of bounds. Now it was UConn's turn to die by the buzzer beater, which is precisely what happened as Christian Laettner hit a jumper as time ran out to give Duke a 79-78 victory.

"I've always wanted to coach in a Final Four," Calhoun said afterward. "But I'll tell you right now, I wouldn't trade this group of kids or the privilege of coaching them for a hundred Final Fours."

To this day, Calhoun remembers George's near steal against Duke more vividly than George's shot against Clemson: "Tate has the ball, and he looks up at me and we're both going to smile because he's just going to hold the ball. He's going to dribble up the court, no one is going to be near him, all the way to the Final Four in Denver. I'm not sure if he took his eyes off it or what, but it just comes out of his hands and it comes close, but it does hit the line. There was a queasy feeling in my stomach after that. I had a more positive feeling about us making the shot against Clemson than I did about Duke not scoring the two points to win.

"But, in retrospect, that may have been a defining moment for us in that it showed we had more work to do. And again, all scripts are not written to come out the way you want. Yeah, the shot against Clemson was phenomenal, but Tate had that ball, he had that ball . . ."

Despite the loss, some seven thousand fans greeted the team at Gampel Pavilion when it returned from New Jersey that evening. What the players and coaches needed at that point was a group hug, which is what the cheering, appreciative crowd provided.

"What made the Dream Season magical was that we had good kids," Calhoun says. "No one seemed to overreact to anything. There were no big egos involved, no big stars. It was really an easy road for a coach. Honestly, I felt less pressure than I have had in the last couple of years. And the reason there was no pressure was because the kids didn't put any on themselves. If someone told them to adjust, they adjusted. We weren't a particularly good offensive team, but we were so devastating defensively. If you couldn't handle the press, then we were going to get you, just like our fast break gets you now.

"You think about the players: Smitty didn't say much. Sellers didn't say much. Lyman didn't say much. Toraino Walker didn't say anything. Nadav said very little. It was one of those teams that just went out and worked."

In four short years, Jim Calhoun had gone from the coach at Northeastern to the consensus National Coach of the Year.

In four short years, UConn had gone from the pits to the pinnacle in the Big East Conference.

In four short years, the University of Connecticut had gotten it done.

"The NIT was the first concrete evidence that UConn basketball had changed," Calhoun says. "That clearly defined us as having a chance to become a national program. The first time that we saw what we had become was the Dream Season.

I can't compare what we went through with the women's success because I wasn't there. But I had never seen so much joy in the state. It was unabated, unbelievable, pure love.

"UConn basketball, from that point on, good or bad, could never be the same. It operates in a different arena now. But the Dream Season was the point that we knew, yes we can."

Where the Elite Meet

While the Dream Season served notice that the UConn men's basketball program had risen to a new level, it provided no guarantees. The proof of a program is in consistency, which was the next challenge. And that was not going to be easy. No longer would UConn be taken lightly by opponents, no longer could UConn ambush unsuspecting teams. Now everyone would be ready for the media darlings from Storrs, pumped up to take them on and bring them down. In addition, there was the little matter of expectation. It is one thing to play well when no one really expects you to win. It is another thing to play well when you are *supposed* to win. The sport may still have been basketball, but, in essence, it was now a whole new game.

"I've never been impressed by someone taking a bunch of freshmen, losing, getting better, getting better, then senior year having a one-shot chance at success, and then starting the whole process all over again," Calhoun says. "I'm impressed by the Dean Smiths of the world, twenty-five wins every year at North Carolina. Nebraska football, vying for the National Championship every year. And that's where we wanted to be."

Still smelling the heady scents of the Dream Season, number-seventeen-ranked UConn opened up the 1990–91 campaign going 12-1, including 3-0 in the Big East. Henefeld was gone, but remaining were Chris Smith, Scott Burrell, Rod Sellers, John Gwynn, Lyman DePriest, Toraino Walker, and Dan Cyrulik.

The fast start, however, was followed by hard times, as UConn lost six straight Big East games. But by the end of the season, the team was back on track, winning six of its final seven in the conference to finish third with a 9-7 mark.

Although UConn was immediately ousted by Georgetown in the Big East Tournament, the 18-10 team was made the number eleven seed in the Midwest Region of the NCAA Tournament. Number six seed LSU, with Shaquille O'Neal, was the first opponent, and UConn won easily, 79-62. UConn also had no trouble with Xavier, defeating them, 66-50, to advance to the Sweet Sixteen for the second year in a row and a rematch with Duke. The venue, the Pontiac Silver Dome, was different, but the result was the same, only more lopsided. UConn lost to the eventual National Champions, 81-67, to finish the season at 20-11, ranking number fifteen.

The following season was very similar. Number-fifteen-ranked UConn again started strong, getting off to an 11-0 start that included victories over Texas, Wake Forest, Illinois, and St. John's. A loss in early January to Villanova was followed by five straight conference wins, good enough for a number five ranking in the national polls and a 16-1 record. And then came the slump, this time a five-game affair. At season's end, UConn stood 18-9 and again took an early first-game exit in the Big East Tournament.

Seeded number nine in the Southeast Region, UConn met number eight Nebraska in the opening-round game and coasted to a twenty-one-point win. It was UConn's third straight appearance in the NCAA Tournament. Ohio State, the number one seed, was up next. The Buckeyes, however, proved to be too much, extending a one-point halftime lead to win in a walk by twenty-three.

"We just weren't that good a team that year," Calhoun says. "The team had accomplished a lot early on and was not ready to handle success. Smitty was starting to think about the pros. Agents started raising their heads for the first time."

Still, the level of consistency Calhoun sought seemed to be building, so much so that he allowed himself to become ever-so-slightly disassociated from some of the basic elements that had been keys to his success. As a result, the program took an unexpected dip in 1992–93, going 15-13 overall, 9-9 in the Big East, losing in the first round of the Big East Tournament, failing to make the NCAA Tournament, and losing in the first round of the NIT to Jackson State.

"People say that was an awful season," Calhoun says. "Well, UConn knows awful seasons, and that was not an awful season. But it was a long way from where we had been. Everything bad that could have happened, happened. Toraino Walker quit the team. Burrell was injured most of the year.

Donyell Marshall had a bad knee. Covington Cormier, who was an All-American junior college player, didn't turn out to be as good as we thought he would be. Richie Ashmeade left the program.

"What that season proved to me was that the same things we did when we were nine and nineteen we should have been doing again. A program doesn't take care of itself. You have to cross all the T's, dot all the I's. I'm much more of a personal coach. I'm a guy who tries to get to people. My practices are psychologically tough. I try and get a player to an edge and then bring him back. I would rather get the kids to care, respond, love each other, play hard than draw good plays. But the fifteen and thirteen year I got a little X's and O's conscious.

"I'm usually involved in every single thing. But I probably wasn't as involved as we got better and better. I didn't get lazy, I was just looking at trying to improve the program in other ways, and we just weren't ready to do that. As a result, the closeness of the team got away a little bit. Kids were doing speaking engagements, they were in demand now because we had been winning so much. Basketball was in prime time. We had to learn how to handle that, and it was a big adjustment."

After the season, Calhoun gathered his staff together and instituted a back-to-basics movement. He barred players from living in apartments off campus and made team breakfasts a mandatory meal. "We assumed all the small, mundane details in their everyday lives," Calhoun says, "so that the people they were most hearing were me, Howie Dickenman, Dave Leitao, Ted Taigen. Those were the voices that were waking them up every single day. Overall, fifteen and thirteen was only a temporary stop to tell us that getting successful had been a hard job and that maintaining success was going to be even more difficult."

Riding a renewed commitment to detail, UConn basketball embarked upon the 1993–94 season resolved to show that the previous year had been an aberration, not a harbinger. Although the team was picked by the Big East coaches to finish fourth in the conference, considerable notice was taken following the shocking outcome of the second regular-season game. Traveling to Charlottesville to meet number-twelve-ranked Virginia, UConn handed the Cavaliers their worst home loss in history, 77-36.

The team continued to play well throughout the season, eventually winning the Big East with a 16-2 record. At the end of the regular season, UConn had not only set a conference record for number of Big East victories in a season and captured the league by a full three games but had also compiled a perfect 15-0 record at home.

After taking the traditionally early exit in the Big East Tournament, UConn entered the NCAA Tournament as the number two seed in the East Regional. In advancing to the Sweet Sixteen, UConn scored an eighteen-point victory over Rider and a twelve-point win against George Washington, both of which were a bit more shaky than the final scores indicate.

In another one of those games that will go down in UConn basketball lore, UConn met the University of Florida at the Miami Arena. With mere seconds remaining, Donyell Marshall missed two free throws that would have assured victory. Instead, the game went into overtime and UConn lost 69-60.

Despite the tough ending, the season marked UConn's

third appearance in the Sweet Sixteen in five years, domina-
tion of the conference, and a return to the upper echelon. It
also offered proof that Calhoun's born-again embrace of the
little things was necessary if good things were going to
happen.

If 1993–94 put UConn back among the nation's top programs, the 1994–95 season seconded the notion, elevating
them to yet another level, to a plateau where the air is rarefied
and elite.

Not only did the team start the year by winning fifteen
straight, post a 13-0 start in the Big East, go 28-5 overall, and
advance to the Elite Eight before losing to National Champion UCLA, but they again did so in dominating fashion.

They ended the season ranked number six, were never
ranked out of the Top 10, and were number one in mid-
February.

They averaged eighty-six points per game during the regular season and almost ninety-eight points per game for four
NCAA Tournament appearances.

They set a school record for wins in a two-year period: fifty-
seven.

They owned the Big East, setting records for winning two
consecutive regular seasons, for most victories in consecutive
seasons, thirty-two, and for number of games in first place,
thirty-six.

"At the end of this past season we were probably the sec-
ond-best team in the country," Calhoun says. "UCLA coach
Jimmy Harrick said it, and I believe we were. And just look at
the last two years, we've lost one game at home. That means if

you have come to thirty-five or thirty-six games, you have only seen us get beat one time.

"The only thing that is missing for us is a National Championship. Final Four? A break here or there, UCLA this year, Duke, and we're there. The theory is if you knock on the door enough times it will open, and I think that will happen. Ray Allen was talking to someone the other day, and he told them, 'It's not me, it's the program. I happen to be the player right now. Whether it be me or Scott Burrell or Chris Smith, somebody fills that role. And there will be someone in the future. You don't know who he is, but he's coming.'

"So now we are at the best level. And we would like to be in or around that level all the time. And we are working really hard at it. I know from whence we came. I know where we are now. And I know how difficult it is going to be to maintain."

Rebuilding:
The Women's Program

While the glass house that is men's basketball at UConn was being constructed pane by pain, the women's program was making equally steady, though much-less-noticed, progress. Unlike Calhoun, who was forced to deal with a myriad of outside problems, Auriemma was able to concentrate almost exclusively on basketball. He did not have to battle the university over academic requirements or players' eligibility. He did not have to crisscross the state reassuring the restless. He did not have to deal with a prying press or impatient public. Instead, away from the glare and external pressure, he could focus on recruiting, coaching, and establishing his program.

Because he had been hired in August and was thus unable to recruit, Auriemma was forced to play the hand that was dealt him his first season. Working with his predecessor's players, he nonetheless was able to finish the 1985–86 season with a 12-15 record that included a school-record four Big East victories. The team also had a school-record seven-game winning streak and was ranked eleventh nationally in field-goal percentage defense (39.6). So there were signs.

Another indication that things were changing had occurred in midseason, when Renée Najarian, a talented six-foot-one junior forward from Wakefield, Massachusetts, transferred to UConn from the University of South Carolina. Although Najarian was not allowed to play upon arrival, she did have two years' eligibility beginning in late December.

Najarian, however, was not the new program's top recruit going into the 1986–87 season. That distinction belonged to Kris Lamb, a highly regarded five-foot-eleven guard from Richmond, Virginia, who had been a Street & Smith High School All-American. Auriemma had become aware of Lamb while he was an assistant at Virginia, and landing her became the program's first recruiting coup. "I always look back at Kris Lamb as being the first key recruit," Dailey says. "She was the first one to take a chance on a program that wasn't really good at the time. And she was coming from Virginia, which was pretty far away then."

Led by Najarian, Lamb, and another freshman, Heidi Robbins, the 1986–87 UConn women went 14-13 to record the school's first winning season in six years. The team also finished tied for fourth in the Big East with a 9-7 record. In addition, Lamb, Najarian, and Robbins all received varying Big East postseason honors.

Based on the measurable strides the program had made in two years, the beginning of the 1987–88 season was eagerly anticipated. But while Auriemma's third season would yield more victories than any other UConn women's team had ever earned, in terms of advancing the program, the season would provide little momentum. The problem was one of chemistry.

Auriemma was confident going into the season. On the recruiting front, the program had landed its two best high school players in school history: Laura Lishness, an athletic guard who was the Player of the Year in Connecticut, and Kerry Bascom, a high school All-American from Epping, New York. Adding the two blue-chippers to a core of Najarian, Lamb, and Robbins offered the potential for a breakthrough season. Although the team compiled a 17-11 record, 9-7 in the Big East, it failed to live up to its promise in Auriemma's eyes.

"There was a sense on that team that it was made up of some of my guys and some of the other coach's people," Auriemma says. "I think it was unfair, but then maybe I didn't do a good job of communicating. The new guys wanted to show that they had ridden in on white horses and were going to build the program, while the older guys were thinking, what are we, chopped liver? He must not have any confidence in us because he is bringing in all these new people.

"I think that was unwarranted because it was the older players that I was counting on that season. The new guys weren't ready yet. But it didn't work out that way. What we had were a lot of people staking out their own turf. Old guys trying to hang on, new guys trying to push them out of the way.

"I think it's part of what every coach goes through when they are building a program. The way some coaches handle it is they just run people off. I'm taking your scholarship, see ya. I don't think you should do that. I think you have to find a way to win with what you have. And we did, we won seventeen games. Was it enjoyable? No. The mix of individuals was just too diverse. You couldn't bring them together. I thought that team could have won twenty, twenty-one games. But they didn't have the intangibles."

After the season, Auriemma set about altering the alchemy. Some marginal players he had taken a chance on were told point-blank that they needed either to change or to find another situation. Some walk-ons were asked to take a hike. "I had Laura Lishness, Kerry Bascom, Kris Lamb, and Heidi Robbins, four guys who wanted to win more than anything," Auriemma says. "Then I had some players who were just going through the motions. And that had to change."

The following season, transformation came in a big way. A 24-6 record, a 13-2 mark in the conference that was accompanied by Big East regular-season and tournament titles, a national ranking (twenty-ninth), and a first-ever invitation to the NCAA Tournament, where UConn lost to La Salle in the first round, 72-63.

Equally encouraging for the program was the fact that people were beginning to pay attention. On February 18, a crowd of 1,860 occupied the Field House for a game with Providence. And over the final three weeks of the season, the team averaged 1,360 fans for home games, which was 1,000 more per game than it had drawn at the beginning of the season.

"I always see the Providence game as a turning point," says associate director of athletic communications Barb Kowal.

"We had so many people at the game that we had to pull the bleachers out on both sides of the Field House, which was a first."

Interest may have been rising, but there was no fever yet, no hint of Huskymania. "I remember we were coming back from Seton Hall after winning the Big East Tournament," Kowal says. "And all the players were talking, wondering, 'Think there will be anyone there? Think there will be anyone to meet the bus?' But when we got to the campus there were maybe six or seven people, a few friends, a couple of roommates. We went into the Field House and a reporter for *The Daily Campus* took a picture of the team and that was it. We had done something big, but we were not recognized like the men had been after they won the NIT the year before."

If chemistry had been the weakness of the 1987–88 team, it was now a strength. The 1988–89 team had no seniors, two sophomores, three juniors, and six talented freshmen. The newcomers included Debbie Baer, Meghan Pattyson, Wendy Davis, and Stacey Wetzel, who as a group would turn out to be the key recruits in the development of the program. "That class put us over the top," Dailey says. "It gave us numbers and versatility. It also gave us the type of kid, the type of work ethic, that would define Connecticut basketball."

"That was the team from my perspective that got Connecticut women's basketball started," Auriemma says. "When that recruiting class arrived, that's when it all began. A lot of it was their personalities and the way they mixed. And then Kerry Bascom had a sophomore year like nobody's ever had. I still think it's the best year anybody's ever had that I coached.

"We didn't have a center. We played all five guys on the

perimeter, and that year we led the country in three-point field-goal percentage [46.3]. We probably shot five or six hundred, had three kids who shot over forty percent. We were just impossible to defend."

Following the season, Auriemma was named Big East Coach of the Year and Bascom Big East Player of the Year. "We go from seventeen and eleven, with only four guys coming back, to twenty-six and six," Auriemma says. "And we could have won a couple of more games. Why? Because now I had all kids that thought the same way."

While the state of Connecticut was fixated on the UConn men's Dream Season during 1989–90, the UConn women enjoyed their second straight year as a top team in the Big East and became a growing concern on the national scene.

The 25-6 team, which finished 14-2 and tied for first in the Big East with Providence, also achieved its first Top 25 national ranking, became the first Big East school to win regular-season titles back to back, and set new attendance records.

For fifteen home games, the team averaged 1,348 fans, which included a crowd of 3,151 for their Gampel Pavilion debut against Georgetown on January 31. That figure would reign for little more than a month, falling when 4,137 turned out to watch the women play and lose to Providence in the Big East Tournament championship game.

Entering the forty-eight-team NCAA Tournament as one of only sixteen seeds, UConn had a bye in the first round to set up a second-round game with Clemson at Gampel Pavilion. While the Clemson men would fall to UConn in the NCAA men's tournament on The Shot, there would be some rendering of the cosmic justice that governed the season in the meeting between the schools' women's teams. Final score, Clemson 61, UConn 59.

Despite the obvious success, Auriemma felt more could have been wrung from the season if his own performance had been better.

"The year before I was very demanding," Auriemma says. "We did things a certain way. Now I had everybody from that team back, and I took things for granted. These guys know what is going on. I don't need to say that again, I don't need to show them that again, I don't need to harp on that again. I don't need to keep an eye on certain things like I used to. Let's get on with it.

"So I let things go, and we won twenty-five games. But we weren't as good. The telling thing was at the end of that year. Meghan Pattyson comes to me, we're having year-end wrapups, and I say to her, 'What do you think, Meg?' And she says to me, 'I think you were a bit of a wuss this year. I think you need to get back to where you were. I don't think you were hard enough on us.'

"Which just goes to show you. People say 'girls.' Well, they're not girls, they're athletes, and she didn't appreciate that I came in that year and took things for granted. Because then the players did. So the following year, I was an SOB the whole season, and look where we went."

The women were in an unfamiliar position going into the 1990–91 season. They were not only supposed to win, they were expected to win, even picked to win. Before the season began, they had become the first Big East women's team to be ranked in a preseason poll, when Street & Smith picked them twenty-fourth. They had also been projected to win the Big East.

There was good reason for the optimism. Returning were Bascom, Big East Player of the Year the past two seasons, Lishness, Baer, Pattyson, Davis, and six-foot-three sophomore Kathy Ferrier, who had made the All Big East Rookie Team. In addition, Orly Grossman, an Israeli with six years' international experience, had joined the team, and freshman redshirt Heidi Law was coming back after missing a year with a stress fracture.

As high as the hopes were—and in the preseason the possible always overshadows the probable—the team was a bit surprised when Auriemma told them on the first day of practice that the goal was going to be the Final Four. "Here is how we are going to do it," Auriemma told his surprised team. "We are going to win the Big East Conference Tournament. We are going to win the regular season."

Out of conference, Auriemma had scheduled Iowa, Auburn, and Purdue, all upper-echelon teams. As expected, this new level of competition proved formidable. Iowa came to Storrs and returned home with a 58-41 victory. UConn went to North Carolina and lost by two points in overtime.

Doubts and red flags rose. Maybe this team wasn't as good as was thought? Maybe the Final Four was a flight of fancy, a hoop dream? Those self-doubts were dispersed in early December, when UConn edged number-two-ranked Auburn, 67-63, to chalk up the program's biggest victory to date.

After Auburn, the team tore through the rest of the regular season, winning fourteen straight at one point and ending up with a number thirteen national ranking based upon a 23-4 record that included a 14-2 mark in the Big East. For the third straight year, the Big East title had been captured, and for the third straight year, attendance climbed. For sixteen home games the team averaged 1,629 fans and set a school and Big East record by drawing 5,420 for a game against Syracuse. What made the attendance jump even more impressive was that it was achieved in spite of the fact that admission was being charged for the first time. Television was also showing interest, and five games had appeared on the New England Sports Network.

After dispatching Villanova, Seton Hall, and Providence in the Big East Tournament, UConn set their sights on making a run in the NCAAs. Although the team would advance to the Final Four, in retrospect Auriemma feels a lack of luck, respect, and experience on his part prevented the team from possibly going all the way.

"I don't think coaches win games," Auriemma says, "but they can sure lose them. Sometimes coaches can screw up a team.

"I had told the team that if we beat Toledo in the first game, which I thought was going to be tough, and it was [81-80], we were going to beat North Carolina State in the next game. They were convinced we were going to kick North Carolina's ass, and they played the best game any team of mine has ever played. And we just destroyed them [82-71].

"Now on Friday, we have practice, and I'm a lunatic. I'm worse than I have been all year because I sense how close we are, and I'm all over them. It gets to the point that they don't even want to be around me. Finally, I tell Chris, get them on the bus, get them away from me.

"Saturday we play Clemson, and I'm a wild man on the sidelines. I want to win this game so bad. And we win [60-57]. So now we're in the Final Four against Virginia, and you know what, I shut down. Oh, we were the life of the party in New Orleans, and we got our work done, but it wasn't the same. My approach to the team leading up to the game and through the first half was not what it should have been. I let them proceed at their own pace, just like I had done the year earlier, and it caught up to us. I didn't have them on the edge. I had spent the whole year pissing them off at the right moment, and now, for that particular game, I let them cruise."

What may have cost UConn that game more than Auriemma's approach was the officiating. In the first few minutes, Bascom was called for two fouls that were noncalls at best. As a result, she had to sit. Another factor was Lishness, who had a subpar game when she most needed to carry the burden.

"We got screwed in that game, no question," Auriemma says. "That happens a lot to us because of, one, where we are located, and two, because I'm a guy in a women's game and they don't like that. You know, only two men have ever won the National Championship, but then women do have the best jobs in the country, so they have the best chance of getting there. So maybe it's a little bit of paranoia on our part. But we didn't get the respect we deserved at that Final Four. I don't think they would have made those same calls on some other kid who was an All-American."

Despite the bad breaks, UConn was only down to Virginia 57-55 with seventeen seconds remaining, but Virginia hit its foul shots in the waning seconds to win 61-55. Auriemma firmly believes that had UConn gotten past Virginia, which had been ranked number one during the season, they would have beaten Tennessee. "Tennessee was big and slow," Auriemma says, "and would not have been able to guard our perimeter people. We could have won the National Championship that year. But you have to get the breaks, you have to be lucky, and we weren't lucky."

Still, as far as the program was concerned, more strides had been made. Going into the NCAA Tournament, UConn had never won an NCAA game. Now it was hanging out in some very fast company: Stanford, Virginia, Tennessee—and Connecticut. It was almost like a "Sesame Street" list. Which one doesn't fit? Except now Connecticut did.

The program had also received valuable national television exposure from its game with Virginia, which had been broadcast on CBS. Even in Connecticut, the UConn women, with their 29-5 record, Final Four appearance, and number four ranking could no longer be ignored. Fans were getting ready to assume a second obsession.

An interesting coincidence regarding the UConn women's rise is that both teams' major advancements in terms of program development occurred the season after the UConn men's program had taken a significant step forward. In 1988, the men won the NIT. In 1988–89, the women won their first Big East title. In 1989–90, the men had their Dream Season. In 1990–91, the women reached their first Final Four.

"I don't think anything happened on the departmental level because of the men," Auriemma says. "But I don't know what the kids were thinking. Maybe they thought that's pretty neat. Because they are all good friends. We probably benefited from all the excitement that went along with their sold-out games and the arena being packed. I think that contributed to people walking past Gampel, seeing the lights on, going inside to see what was happening, and liking what they saw."

Just as the men had learned following the Dream Season, the women discovered that success does not guarantee more success and that sustaining a program at a high level is probably more difficult than getting it there. The next two seasons would drive that point home.

The 1991–92 season was one of passage. Gone were Bascom and Lishness, the two best players in the program's history to that point. Arriving were Pam Webber and Rebecca Lobo, who would not only become the best player in the program's history but would be the best female player in the entire nation her senior year.

Although Lishness and Bascom were no longer around, the team still had the Baer-Davis-Pattyson class and a whole lot of experience. What it didn't have was the magic of the previous season or an answer to the University of Miami, which dominated the conference, finishing 18-0. On the year, UConn went 23-11 and tied for second in the Big East at 13-5. They lost to Miami in the Big East Tournament championship game and were ousted in the second round of the NCAA Tournament. A respectable season to be sure, but one that did little to advance the program.

If 1991–92 was a season of passage, 1992–93 was a season of painful transition: 18-11, 12-6 in the Big East, out in the first round of the NCAA Tournament.

"We had lost Kerry and Laura, and now we lose Debbie Baer, Meghan Pattyson, and Wendy Davis. So in two years we had lost all five kids that started for us for four years," Auriemma says. "And we are in deep trouble because all we have are Rebecca and Pam Webber, and they are sophomores. We have those two and three freshmen in the starting lineup. I mean, Pam and Kim Better at guards, and neither shot over thirty percent, and they played thirty minutes a game. If it wasn't for Jen Rizzotti and Jamelle Elliott having good freshmen years, it would have been a really tough year."

In Chris Dailey's mind, the 1992–93 season was, in a way, payback time for the consistency and experience the team had enjoyed in previous seasons: "You have to remember that the kids who were juniors and seniors on that team had not gotten a lot of playing time because we had Laura and Kerry and Wendy and Meghan and Debbie, and they got the majority of time. The reason that group had been so successful was because they had gotten a lot of time as freshmen and sophomores. The kids coming after them didn't get that. But I think that year we probably got more out of that team than any team we have ever had. We really accomplished a lot. I don't think we realized how much we got out of that team until the following year."

All the 1993–94 team did was go 30-3, win the Big East (17-1) regular season and tournament, advance to the Elite Eight of the NCAA Tournament, and raise the UConn women's basketball program to the highest level.

The team started 7-0 before traveling to the West Coast to meet powerful Stanford, where they were defeated 94-75. "We lost that game because Stanford was just better than us,"

Auriemma says. "But we played well enough that night to beat everyone else we had on our schedule."

While the loss to Stanford was to be expected, the team's second defeat of the season, to Seton Hall, was not. And, in fact, probably could have been avoided.

"I took that game to teach them a lesson," Auriemma says. "I went into that game worried that we had come back from California with the wrong mind-set. We had started slipping. We were playing kind of haphazard. When we went to Seton Hall, I could sense that something wasn't quite right. We looked tired, had no life.

"At halftime, I decided I was going to give them about seven or eight minutes to see if we could generate some enthusiasm. About the twelve-minute mark, I started yanking the big guys: Rebecca out, Kara Wolters sit down, Jen, Jamelle. And I let the string play out. I thought we needed to lose by thirty or forty, so I hoped they would really pound us. But they couldn't. But my guys felt the sting of sitting there watching them celebrate, watching them win. I just let that kind of sink in. We finally lose by twenty, and when we get on the bus, I say, 'I don't want to hear a sound on the way back.' We came home, and I felt really good about our team. I knew we wouldn't lose another game in the Big East."

In the NCAA Tournament, UConn drew North Carolina, a team that proved to be too strong and too fast. The defeat, however, was significant in a historical sense. It would be the last game the UConn women would lose in more than a year.

Pat Meiser-McKnett, the former Penn State women's basketball coach and UConn associate athletic director, was an interested observer with a front-row seat as the construction of the women's program was undertaken. She sums up the process this way: "The first player was Kris Lamb, and they wrapped a group of kids around her. Then it was Kerry Bascom and Laura Lishness, and they wrapped a group of kids around them. Then there was Wendy Davis, Debbie Baer, Meghan Pattyson, and they wrapped kids around them. And then it was Rebecca. And now it's Nykesha Sales. It's perfect. It's absolutely perfect. It's an incredible picture of how to build a program."

Perfect: 35 and Oh!

In 1994–95, Connecticut women's basketball climbed until it ran out of summits. Only after the team had won the National Championship and gone undefeated did the season end. But there was an irony to the stunning accomplishment, one that most people measured in terms of the thirty-five victories. Winning was not the obsession. Winning was not the day-in, day-out goal. Winning was, in fact, irrelevant. The guiding force, the motivating factor, was not perfection, it was performance.

"If you looked at the league before the season, you saw that we had everybody back from a thirty and three team *and* we had added Nykesha Sales," Auriemma says. "Anybody that was close to us had lost a lot and didn't have a Nykesha. We are going to win every game in our league if we play to a certain level. So winning became not such a big deal. Instead, it became the *way* we play. The mind-set became, forget about the wins, those are going to take care of themselves. We're going to win twenty or twenty-five games just because we are really good. How we win those games, though, and how far we go in the tournament will depend upon our approach. We never talked about winning."

Auriemma began instilling his performance-based philosophy on the team's preseason trip to Europe.

"They'd say, Coach, who we playing? I'd say, I have no idea. Who do they have? I have no idea. What defense? I have no idea. How we going to play them? Well, we're going to do this, this, this. Let's go. Then, after ten minutes, okay, here's what they're doing. Here's what we can do, okay, let's finish it off.

"And we came back with that approach. Coach, what do they do? Does it matter? No. Then let's go play. And that was the attitude they took throughout the whole season. That it doesn't matter what anybody does; if we play to our abilities, no one can beat us. Playing at a certain level was our goal. And whenever we didn't reach that level, everyone was pissed.

"I had a coach in the league tell me, 'People don't understand how good you guys really are. You've been beating everyone by thirty-five, but it could have been fifty because your guys are only playing twenty-five minutes a game.' And he was right. People would ask me why we were diving on loose balls, why we were jumping into the press row when we were up thirty-five. Because the score was irrelevant. We were not playing for the final score. We knew we were going to win. But we had to play at a certain level."

The criteria to measure performance became a series of

goals for each game, goals that when considered individually meant little in the overall scheme but when taken collectively meant everything.

"The little goals became our barometer because they are all the things that lead to winning," Auriemma says. "We'd have this sheet up there with twelve goals. The ones we hit would get highlighted. If we only got six, that means in six other areas in which we tried to be good, we were lousy, regardless of the score.

"We played California and were up twenty-five-nothing at one point. The final score was like ninety-nine to fifty-two. The sheet after the game said we got nine of our goals. But I didn't have to look at the sheet because I knew the first ten minutes was as good basketball as anyone could play at any level at any time. It would be impossible to be better than that. But then sometimes we would beat somebody bad and you'd think something didn't look right and you'd look at the sheet and realize, yeah, we were awful. We wanted to win because we were really good, not because the other team wasn't. We wanted the other team going home saying the reason they lost wasn't because they sucked but because Connecticut was really good."

During the 1989–90 season, Auriemma had eased up, taken too many things for granted, and this had resulted in an attitude that hurt the team. In 1994–95, he was determined to reap the rewards of that painful object lesson. "The past season we had been thirty and three. And I said to myself, I'm not going to make that same mistake twice. I'm getting on these guys right from the start, and I did. But we enjoyed it because I was on them the right way. And we had the right kids."

The first step on the journey to a place called perfection was taken in Europe. In mid-August, the team took a twelve-day, five-game trip that included stops in Belgium, France, and Italy. While Auriemma used the trip to begin ingraining his philosophy—*it ain't what they do, it's what we do*—the working vacation had another enormous benefit. Chemistry. Coaches always like to take an extended road trip early in the season because being away with just teammates serves to create a bond. The European sojourn had just that effect on the UConn women. A closeness so vital to their success was forged during the four-victory excursion. "Chemistry is a funny thing," Chris Dailey says. "You know when you don't have it, but you don't know how to fix it. But when you have it, it's special."

If there was a word that described the outlook going into the 1994–95 season, it was optimism. But this wasn't the usual preseason dose of feel-good follies founded in what might be possible. This optimism was based in cold, hard reality. The previous season, the women had gone 30-3, finished the season ranked third in the country, led the nation in field-goal percentage defense (33.7 percent), and were second in field-goal shooting percentage (50.5). And they were all back, nine letter winners, including four starters, plus the best high school player in the country. On paper, and in sneakers, the lineup was impressive:

Rebecca Lobo, a consensus All-American and National Player of the Year candidate.

Kara Wolters, a six-foot-seven post player who had improved dramatically over the summer.

Jen Rizzotti, one of the best point guards in the nation.

Jamelle Elliott, a dribbling definition of the word toughness.

Pam Webber, a solid performer with three years' experience.

Carla Berube, an aggressive offensive boost off the bench.

And freshman Nykesha Sales, a high school All-American and *USA Today* National Player of the Year.

The season opened with a devastating 107-27 victory over Morgan State. Three more wins followed, the closest game being a twenty-five point squeaker. In early December, the first test of the season arrived via an away game at North Carolina State. Not only did UConn ace the exam, 98-75, but in doing so scored the most points ever allowed by a North Carolina State team at home. The victory, coupled with a Stanford loss, elevated the UConn women to the number two spot in the polls behind Tennessee. Over the next six games, things progressed from simply dominating to downright frightening, the machine scoring 101, 99, 100, 103, 98, and 104 points while posting victory margins of 59, 54, and 47 points.

On January 13, Seton Hall came calling, the unconvinced media billing the game as a serious challenge to the 12-0 women from Storrs. Seton Hall had been the last Big East team to defeat UConn—even though Auriemma may have been the Hall's MVP in that contest—and were ranked number nineteen. The final score was 80-36, the only concern being the dislocated pinkie Lobo suffered toward the end of the game.

While North Carolina State and Seton Hall had proved to be paper threats, there was no arguing that the next game on the schedule would go a long way in determining just how good this UConn team really was.

If January 16 were not already a holiday in Connecticut—Martin Luther King Day—it would have been necessary to declare it so. Certainly little work was going to get done with number-one-ranked Tennessee meeting number-two-ranked UConn before a national audience on ESPN. Tennessee was 16-0 and featured twelve high school All-Americans on its roster, including ten returning letter winners from a team that had gone 31-2 the previous season. Whether UConn (12-0) was up to the challenge was to be decided, but there was no doubt that the sellout Gampel Pavilion crowd of 8,241 was emotionally prepared. Some had paid scalpers as much as $80 for an $8 ticket. The media had also turned out in force. Eyeing the 150-member media contingent, Auriemma cracked, "We didn't get that many *fans* here for my first game."

The atmosphere was charged at the opening tip. The two teams came out snorting intensity, Tennessee taking an early 6-5 lead. But then Lobo dropped a three and Rizzotti made a three-point play and UConn had a ten-point run and 15-6 advantage. At the intermission, the score was 41-33, UConn.

The battle continued in the second half. With just over nine minutes remaining, UConn's lead was five and everyone in the building was thinking, here they come. Auriemma signaled for a time-out to stem the gathering momentum. In the

sideline huddle he gave one of those they-put-their-makeup-
on-one-eye-at-a-time speeches and then sent his team back
out onto the floor along with Lobo, who had been sitting in
foul trouble. Over the next five minutes, Lobo shot, passed,
and rebounded the team into a 64-53 lead before finally foul-
ing out with 4:52 remaining. As she walked to the bench,
another of those "here-they-come" feelings swept through
the crowd, which was seeing but still not believing. Proof that
this team was not a one-woman show became clear in the
closing minutes, as Wolters and Elliott hit baskets and then
Rizzotti and Elliott made two free throws each to clinch the
77-66 UConn victory.

At the buzzer, Elliott threw the ball high into the air as the
players spilled out onto the floor, eventually collapsing into
what would become one of their trademark piles. The crowd
was jubilant, chanting "We're number one" and refusing to
leave until after the players had come back out for an encore.
For years, the women couldn't draw a crowd, now they
couldn't get rid of one. "This is one of the toughest places
we've played," Tennessee coach Pat Summitt said. "That kind
of atmosphere and support gives them a sixth-player effect.
And it's the same for the men and the women, which makes
them unique."

Despite having to sit in foul trouble and playing with a
broken right pinkie finger that was in a soft splint, Lobo had
thirteen points, eight rebounds, and five blocks. But she had
help. Rizzotti not only handled the Tennessee pressure all
afternoon but also had seventeen points, five steals, and four
assists, while Wolters recorded a game-high eighteen points.
"Rebecca Lobo is the most versatile post player we've faced

and brings lots of confidence to their team," Summitt said. "But they're not just Rebecca Lobo, and I think they understand that."

Although the UConn women would be ranked number one in a matter of hours, and although they had just beaten Tennessee in convincing fashion, there were still doubters. Tennessee was tired from travel, a Saturday night game in Alabama—their third in five days—and flight delays. UConn had simply caught Tennessee at home at a good time. "Our problem wasn't physical," Summitt said. "The problem was Connecticut was more than we were mentally ready to handle."

In a state that bills itself as "The Land of Steady Habits," many remained suspicious of suddenly being the dog with the changing view. Running at the front of the pack was something that happened to the other guys. This would take some getting used to.

On January 17, the UConn women were voted number one, becoming not only the first UConn team ever to earn that distinction but the first women's team from the Big East Conference to do so. That afternoon, the team practiced for their game the next day against Boston College. "I'll wake up tomorrow with a smile on my face," Lobo had said in the locker room after the Tennessee game. "But in practice tomorrow I'll go back to being the worst post player in the country." She was being facetious, but there was truth in the jest. There was no way Auriemma was going to ease up now.

Although an emotional letdown might have been expected after the Tennessee game, the team stayed focused, winning three straight Big East contests. Probably the most contentious episode during the period involved Auriemma. Following a very physical game with Boston College, Auriemma questioned the Eagles' rough style of play and the officials that allowed it. After being privately taken to the woodshed by UConn athletic director Lew Perkins, Auriemma apologized.

On the Saturday afternoon of January 28, the nation was treated to a men's and women's basketball doubleheader on CBS featuring the University of Connecticut and the University of Kansas. Going into the game, both UConn teams were undefeated. Afterward, only the UConn women were blemish-free. The number-two-ranked UConn men ran into a Kansas team that could do no wrong on its way to a dominating 88-59 victory.

The UConn women had played the first game, wanting to prove to the naysayers that they could win a big game on the road. Midway through the first half, the two teams were close, but then UConn went on a late run to grab a twelve-point advantage at the break. UConn's lead continued to ebb and flow in the second half, as Kansas gained energy from the Kemper Arena crowd that had grown to almost 17,000. With less than three minutes remaining, UConn's lead had shrunk to 86-84 and the scent of upset hung heavy in the building. But then UConn hit six free throws down the stretch to escape with a 97-87 win that was a lot closer than the numbers.

Rizzotti and Sales had twenty-one points each, while Lobo provided twenty-five points and twelve rebounds. "I think we responded well and held up to the pressure," Lobo said afterward. "It will only help us down the line."

Now 17-0, UConn faced nine straight Big East games

against teams they had dominated the first time through the conference schedule. Your run-of-the-mill, undefeated, top-ranked team might have had trouble with focus at this point. But not the UConn women because the opponent was now only incidental. Performance was the real foe. And the remainder of the regular season passed in a blitz of blowouts, the closest margin of victory being twenty-two points on two occasions.

There are few things more dangerous than a competitive media situation in which the reporters have time to kill and space to fill. As the women entered the Big East Tournament, a train of thought began to emerge in the media that suggested the best thing that could happen to the UConn women was to lose a game before the NCAA Tournament began. The rationale was that it would relieve the pressure of being undefeated. The players and coaches found the concept absurd.

Going into the Big East Tournament, the women were 26-0 and still number one. They had become the first conference team, men or women, to complete a season undefeated and over the past two years were 35-1 in league play. As anticipated, they overwhelmed the opposition, capturing a record fourth Big East Tournament title. The only source of concern to emerge from the three-game rout fest was an injury to Rizzotti. The feisty point guard had strained a tendon in her elbow following a collision in the second half of the championship game with Seton Hall.

"If you are not careful, your strengths can become your weaknesses," Auriemma is fond of telling his players. Was this a case in point? Was the pursuit of goals becoming so important that common sense was being sacrificed? Rizzotti had been injured recklessly sacrificing her body in a cause that was already won. Could this lack of discretion, this blind allegiance to performance, be the chink in the women's armor? Fortunately, Rizzotti had ten days between the end of the Big East Tournament and the start of the NCAAs to recover, which she did. But what if?

That Rizzotti had sufficient days to recover was a matter of good timing. That UConn would play its first two games in the NCAA Tournament at Gampel Pavilion was a matter of earned opportunity, the team being the number one seed in the East Regional. That UConn would also play Sweet Sixteen and Elite Eight games in Storrs should they continue to advance was a matter of flat-out fate. UConn was not, however, alone in this regard. Tennessee was in exactly the same situation. But even having four potential games at home was no guarantee. In 1994, Stanford had been in that situation and lost to Purdue in the West Regional final.

Maine was first up and first down, losing 105-75 as UConn reached the hundred-point plateau for the seventh time during the season. UConn was now 30-0 and counting.

Carol Alfano, coach of Virginia Tech, summed up her team's performance against UConn in the second round with the help of some down-home philosophy: "Sometimes you're the windshield," she moaned more than crooned, "sometimes you're the bug. We were the bug." Final score: Windshield 91, Bug 45.

UConn's game against Alabama in the East Regional semifinals was kind of like watching an old movie. The setting was the same, Gampel Pavilion. The main characters were the same, Lobo et al. The plot was the same, action-adventure. The ending was the same, UConn 87, Alabama 56. And roll the credits: Elliott, Rizzotti, Wolters, Lobo, Sales. . . .

While the semis had proved to be a rerun, the East Regional final against Virginia was anything but a twice-told tale. The game turned out to have more suspense, more drama, more tension, more twists and turns than a John Grisham story line.

Auriemma was a wreck going into the game. Virginia was never just another game for him, though he tried to make it so. He had come to Connecticut from Virginia. He had worked under Virginia coach Debbie Ryan. For Auriemma, playing Virginia was akin to the small-town kid returning home after making it big. But this time, more than ego and pride were riding on the outcome. It would be the last game in Gampel Pavilion for Rebecca Lobo and Pam Webber, and Auriemma did not want their curtain call to be a teary farewell. And then, of course, there was the small matter of advancing to the Final Four and maintaining their 32-0 record. And if that were not enough motivation, revenge was also lurking about, Virginia having defeated UConn in the 1991 Final Four, 61-55.

The players may have picked up on Auriemma's jittery vibes. "That was the first game that anyone on our team had doubts in their mind that we were going to win," Lobo would later admit.

The game had a *Tale of Two Cities* opening half. At the ten-minute mark, UConn was up, 29-10. At the half, the score was 44-37, Virginia. It was the first time that UConn had been behind at halftime all season, and to make matters worse, they had gotten into this position by not only squandering a big lead but by losing their composure as well. "You can't play any better than we did in the first ten minutes," Auriemma said. "You can't play any worse that we did in the last ten minutes."

Outwardly, there was no panic in the locker room. Inwardly, there was a lot of digging going on, a lot of searching for something deep down inside.

The second half was furious and physical. With 12:43 remaining, UConn tied the score at forty-nine. With 4:39 left, UConn had what appeared to be a safe 66-57 lead. But then Virginia fought back to 66-63 with 2:05 to go. Points were now at a premium. Lobo and Sales missed jumpers, Wolters and Lobo made big blocks. Then came the defensive play of the game. With 19.6 seconds remaining and Virginia coming out of a time-out after having set up a three-point play, UConn denied the inbounds pass, forcing a five-second violation. Elliott was subsequently fouled, and her free throw gave UConn a four-point advantage. Lobo then put the icing on the victory by blocking a last-minute three-point attempt. The UConn women were now 33-0 and headed for the Final Four in Minneapolis.

For Auriemma, however, there was little joy, tremendous relief, and tears in his eyes. It was, he says, the first time he has ever cried after a game. Before departing for the Final Four, he told his team: "Everyone else is going to Minneapolis to win the National Championship. We're going there to make history."

Although UConn was now 33-0 and a seven-and-a-half-point favorite to defeat Stanford in the semifinals, there were many who said the game was actually a toss-up because of Stanford's superior depth. Stanford did indeed have twelve high school All-Americans on its roster. What they did not have, however, was anyone to guard Wolters, who scored a game-high thirty-one points. Wolters's output, combined with that of Elliott (twenty-one) and Lobo (seventeen), out-scored Stanford's front court, 69-16. The trio also held Stanford All-American Kate Starbird to two points in twenty-six minutes. In the process, UConn defeated Stanford, 87-60, the largest victory margin in the fourteen-year history of the women's Final Four.

UConn's decisive triumph, coupled with Tennessee's easy win over Georgia, set up the rematch everyone had been hoping for: UConn-Tennessee for the National Championship. UConn over Tennessee for a forever piece of perfection. This time there would be no veiled excuses, no innuendo about the schedule, being tired, airport delays, injuries, or home-court advantage. With a national television audience tuned in for the late Sunday afternoon game on CBS, they threw the ball up. It would be a very long time before UConn and its supporters would come down from what followed.

The last time he had been to the Final Four, Auriemma had, in his own words, "shut down." He had allowed the players to proceed at their own pace. He had failed to keep them on edge psychologically. But he had learned from his mistakes. Now he ranted and raved on the sidelines, kept everyone focused in the locker room.

"I had them convinced we were the best team in the country," Auriemma says, "but that Tennessee was going to beat us by twenty points if we didn't do this and this. So I had them afraid of the right things. We better box out or they are going to kill us on the boards. We better get back on defense or they are going to run it right down our throats. We better be tough inside. I had them thinking along those lines. We just have to be tougher than them because they fancy themselves as the toughest, the strongest, the most intense, mentally tough team in America. And we better go out and kick their ass because they are not going to fall apart in the championship game."

With a national television audience looking on, larger than the one tuned to the Phoenix Suns–San Antonio Spurs NBA game, the contest quickly became a test of wills. Lobo had six of UConn's first twelve points, when suddenly she was whistled for three fouls in ninety-four seconds and forced to spend the last twelve minutes of the half on the bench. To UConn fans it was like Kerry Bascom all over again. To make matters worse, Rizzotti and Sales also had three fouls in the half, and Wolters had two. But try as they might, Tennessee could not fully capitalize on their huge advantage and led by only six points at the half.

Auriemma actually felt good going into the locker room. Tennessee had gotten all the breaks, his team had performed poorly, yet they were only down six. His halftime talk came down to a simple fact of life: "If we out-rebound them in the second half, we will win the game." At the first dead-ball time-out in the second half, Summitt checked the statistics and found UConn had a 12-3 rebounding edge, a statistic that would grow to 25-15 by the end of the game.

With 11:32 left to play and Tennessee leading, 52-46, Rebecca Lobo did what an All-American and the National Player of the Year is supposed to do: She took over the game. Over the next four minutes, Lobo scored eight of the team's nine points, hitting four of five shots, to cut Tennessee's lead to 58-55. Then, with UConn leading 65-61, Lobo closed the game with two huge rebounds and three free throws to nail down a 70-64 victory and the National Championship.

"I don't know what came over me," Lobo said afterward. "Before the game I just had a feeling we were going to win, and that is what made it so hard to sit on the bench in the first half. . . . In the second half, I just wanted to play and I got the opportunity. It was a feeling like, they aren't going to take another chance away from me."

In winning, UConn not only brought the first basketball National Championship to Connecticut but also joined the 1986 Texas team (34-0) as the only unbeaten National Champions. "We didn't set out to be perfect," Auriemma says, "but when they talk about Connecticut basketball in 1995, they are going to say we were perfect."

There was, of course, joy and relief and laughter and tears in the aftermath. The President of the United States would call the locker room, thousands would greet the team on its arrival home, a huge parade through the streets of Hartford would be held, politicians would issue proclamations, the White House would extend an invitation, national television talk shows would call.

As for the Connecticut women's basketball program, it not only rose to a new level but set a new standard. Ten years earlier, a brash guy with a big smile had told a search committee he could win and make them proud. And he had done just that. He had gotten it done.

Rebecca Lobo

Rebecca Lobo had always been a star. Growing up she had been consensus All-Driveway, All-Playground, All–Junior High, All–Summer Camp, All-State. And all along the way, people had patted her on the back and said wonderful things, and her confidence had seemingly become complete as her game blossomed. Or had it? Did she really possess the self-assurance she projected? Did she really have the unyielding blind faith in her abilities that everyone assumed she had? Did she really want the ball with the game on the line, or could she just not hide from it? Despite all the winning, was she a winner?

Lobo had come to UConn as a franchise-caliber recruit in 1991–92. On an experienced, senior-dominated team that had gone to the Final Four the previous year, she put together a fine freshman debut, coming off the bench to average 7.9

rebounds and 14.3 points and was the unanimous choice for Big East Rookie of the Year. The team had gone 23-11, been invited to the NCAA Tournament for the fourth straight year, tied for second in the Big East (13-5), and lost in the conference championship game. Lobo had been important to the team, but not the key component. She had enjoyed the luxury of making the transition to college without being immediately placed under a great deal of pressure.

But then came graduation and the departure of senior leadership and, along with these, the loss of Rebecca Lobo's comfort zone. On a team that now included one senior, three juniors—none of whom were starters—two sophomores, and four freshmen, she was suddenly shoved to the forefront. Instead of just fitting in, she would now be the one around whom the team would be blended, the one on whose performance they would ultimately succeed or fail. But was the nineteen-year-old ready for the challenge, or would the weighty responsibility conjure up demons whispering words of self-doubt: "Am I as good as everyone says?" "Can I handle this?"

"Rebecca learned a real valuable lesson her sophomore year," Auriemma says. "She learned what it was like to have to carry a team. At that point she was making a transition from being a freshman. Her first year it was, I'll let Wendy and Meghan do it, they've been to a Final Four. They know what's going on. I'll just come along for the ride. Now she's a sophomore, and she looks around and says, whoa, now I have to get it done. And that's when the doubts started to come up. So I brought her in and told her, hey, the stakes have changed, pal. We're playing for something here. And I went through her whole history.

"Ever win a state championship in high school? No.

"You played AAU, ever win a National Championship, a gold medal? No.

"Played on a sports festival team in California, win the gold? No.

"Played with the Junior National Team, you win it? No.

"You've been here a year and a half now, your first year was the only year we didn't win the Big East championship in the last four years.

"What am I trying to tell you? Whatever you have been doing, your way doesn't work. There's a ceiling here you need to break through. I'm going to show you how to do it, and you have to understand it's not going to be easy. But if you want to get to where you tell me you want to go, then you need to get through this. You need to make some changes in the way you approach the game. It can't be this 'If we win we win, if we don't we don't.' You have to play for a reason, for a purpose. You have to make sure we win because that is what has been thrust upon you. You have to take the last shot. You have to get the big rebound. You have to block the shots. Why? Because if you are counting on someone else to do it, it may not get done. And if you don't, then you are going to be labeled 'can't win.' The other players aren't going to be labeled."

That same night against Seton Hall, Lobo had twenty-seven points, sixteen rebounds, and seven blocks (the latter of which tied a school record she later broke), and UConn won, 72-53. From that point in late February, the team won seven of eight games. During that period, Lobo reached double figures in points and rebounds six times, averaging 20.5 points, 12 rebounds, and 4.8 blocks.

"It was a heart-to-heart meeting," Lobo remembers, "and very constructive. I had gotten a little frustrated for several reasons, and Coach was right in what he said I needed to do. I picked up the intensity and got a little mean."

"It was a process," Auriemma says. "She was able to gear herself up, but if she had to do it too many times in a row, she still didn't have that ability. Being able to do it day after day after day, that came her junior year."

Fast-forward:

If there was a player who apparently had nothing to prove going into the National Championship game with Tennessee, it was Rebecca Lobo: She was the Naismith Player of the Year, Associated Press National Player of the Year, United States Basketball Writers National Player of the Year, College Sports Magazine National Player of the Year, Women's Basketball News Service National Player of the Year, Big East Conference Player of the Year, ECAC Conference Player of the Year, Kodak First Team All-American, Associated Press First Team All-American, and United States Basketball Writers First Team All-American.

Yet Auriemma was concerned about her, worried about what effect the mounting pressure might have on her. One of the litmus tests of superstars is the ability to lead their team to a championship, to perform their best at the biggest moment. And now that time was at hand for Rebecca Lobo. For UConn to win the National Championship and finish 35-0,

Lobo was going to have to have what Auriemma called a "Steve Young kind of day."

"You're player of the year, MVP," Auriemma thought, "but know what, you have this *one* chance to show everyone that those things are true. If you play bad, everything you have done for the last six months is down the tubes. No one is going to believe it. They're not going to remember it."

After she was called for three quick fouls in the first half, Auriemma was forced to sit Lobo. As she sat on the bench near him, Auriemma wondered if Lobo could recover in the second half. Would she be able to take advantage of whatever opportunity presented itself, or would all that she had accomplished be diminished in defeat? And what of the demons? Had they been completely banished, or were they simply hibernating, waiting for the right moment to awaken? With everything on the line, Lobo went back into the game in the second half.

"We want her to want the ball," Rizzotti said. "We want her to make the game-winning shot. We want her to win the game for us. That's what she's supposed to do."

Lobo did what was expected. Under intense pressure, she performed brilliantly:

She made a post-up move with 11:32 left and got an easy layup.

She scored on a drive a few plays later.

She hit an eighteen-foot jumper with 9:03 remaining.

She scored again with 7:40 on the clock from the wing.

Five shots, four baskets, eight of UConn's nine points, and now her team was within three, 58-55.

In the closing minutes, Lobo added two big rebounds and

three free throws. She was named NCAA Final Four Most Outstanding Player. "I just felt really confident," Lobo said afterward. "I felt I could take the game into my own hands."

"She made that post-up move and buried those two jumpers," Auriemma says, "and that was it. That is what won the game. If she doesn't make those three shots, then we are done. After it was over, to her, I think it was, 'I've made it.' Not that I've won the National Championship but that I've gotten to the point where I don't have to worry about all these self-doubts. I'm as good as everyone says I am.

"More than anything else," Auriemma says, "I walked away from that game thinking, Rebecca Lobo, she's come the full cycle. In the biggest showcase of her life, she rose up and got it done."

Rebecca Rose Lobo was born in Hartford, Connecticut, on October 6, 1973, but grew up in Southwick, Massachusetts. Southwick is a two-and-a-half-square-mile jag that juts into Connecticut along its otherwise straight northern border with Massachusetts. Historically, Southwick was noted for being the home of Amasa Holcomb, who manufactured the first celestial telescope, and Cyrus Field, who was responsible for the first telegraph cable being laid across the Atlantic. But truth be told, since the mid-1800s the town of about eight thousand had been in a bit of a slump—until Lobo.

Ruth Ann and Dennis Lobo, public school educators from nearby Granby, Connecticut, moved to Southwick when Rebecca, the youngest of their three children, was one year old. Jason Lobo, who is six years Rebecca's senior, grew to six-foot-eleven, played for Dartmouth, and is now a lawyer. Rachel, who is three years older, played and now coaches basketball at Salem State College.

From third grade on, Lobo was the tallest kid in her class, finally topping off at six-foot-four. Early on, her first love was baseball, but she began to focus on basketball in the fifth grade. She wanted to play in a town recreation league that year, but when only five girls signed up, the team was canceled. She got to play anyway, however, when Ruth Ann insisted she be allowed to play on one of the boys' teams. By the following year, she was drawing attention at developmental camps, where coaches were predicting she had all the qualities necessary to become a special player.

At Southwick-Tolland Regional High School Lobo played basketball, of course, but also participated in softball and track and was All-Western Massachusetts in field hockey. In her very first basketball game as a freshman, Lobo scored thirty-two points. By the end of her final game as a senior, she had scored 2,710 points, to become the Massachusetts all-time high school scoring leader, male or female.

Lobo broke the state career scoring record in February of her senior year by hitting for fifty-five points on twenty-six of thirty-eight shooting. She also had twenty-eight rebounds. Her reaction to the milestone was typical Lobo: "It's a big relief. From now on everybody will be concerned with whether we win, not how many points I score or my average."

As impressive as the fifty-five-point performance was, it was not her highest offensive output of the season. A few days earlier, Lobo had scored sixty-two points. Asked how she felt about that, she responded, "Embarrassed. I mean, this is a team game."

Southwick girls' basketball coach Jim Vincent believed
Lobo to have "more natural talent than anybody" he had ever
coached, including boys. One of his few complaints was that
she was too unselfish, too ready to pass rather than shoot. "I
felt all my teammates had worked as hard in practice as I did,"
Lobo reasoned, "and so they deserved to get recognition
too."

What impressed Vincent more than Lobo's athletic prowess
was her demeanor. "She demonstrates such great sportsman-
ship on and off the court that members of the other team
even look up to her," Vincent said. "I have never seen her get
down on herself or her teammates."

In her senior year, Lobo averaged almost thirty-seven
points, twenty rebounds, and six blocks. She became such a
star that opponents would ask for her autograph after games,
and she often received standing ovations from the other
team's fans.

But high school was not just a series of heady high fives.
Summers kept the budding superstar humble. Throughout
her teens, she worked in the nearby tobacco fields. The work
was hard, hot, and dirty. The pay was based on the amount of
work you did. Lobo consistently set records.

"Rebecca has the best self-discipline of anyone I know,
whether it's in athletics or academics or her musical pursuits
[saxophone]," says Ruth Ann. "When she makes a commitment, she gives it her all."

Coming out of high school, Lobo was considered the number two recruit in America and the number one center. She
was Gatorade Player of the Year and a First Team All-American selection by Street & Smith, *Parade* magazine, and *USA*

Today. She drew interest from three hundred colleges and was actively recruited by one hundred. Eventually, she pared her choices to five: Notre Dame, Northwestern, Richmond, Virginia, and Connecticut.

Chris Dailey had seen Lobo play and was intrigued by the way she acted on the court. She liked the way she supported and treated her teammates. Dailey made UConn's initial contact in September of Lobo's junior year and felt they connected right off. Although Dailey and Auriemma pursued the relationship after that, they did so cautiously.

"We didn't bombard her with phone calls," Dailey says. "We stayed in touch with her throughout her senior year. She came to a number of games here and on the road. One game she and her dad came and didn't even call for tickets. They just wanted to come and watch without being recruited. That said a lot about her and the way she looked at the process. Rebecca was not the kind of kid that got caught up in all the glamour of recruiting. She was more into trying to find out for herself. Obviously, we knew she was at the game, everyone in the building did, but she did not want everyone to ooh and ah over her all the time."

On her official visit, Lobo stayed with Meghan Pattyson.

"Rebecca and I had one of those things where you just click," Pattyson says. "She has a very sarcastic, dry sense of humor, and we would just laugh all the time. Sometimes you know when you connect with someone because you say something and no one else picks it up but that person. Well, we would do that all the time. The Saturday night of her visit, we just sat around in the apartment, Rebecca, myself, Stacey Wetzel, and Pam Rothfuss [another player]. I remember someone brought up the expression 'Jesus H. Christ.' Rebecca wondered what the H stood for. And Pam honestly thought it stood for Henry.

"I thought she would come here when she left. I couldn't imagine her going anywhere else. And I hoped so because I really liked her and wanted to be friends with her. And it had nothing to do with basketball. I just knew this was the place for her because she just fit in really well."

"I tried to keep an open mind the whole time when I was being recruited," Lobo says. "But I think I was always leaning toward the University of Connecticut. My parents really didn't want me to come here, so it was hard balancing those two things. When I took my official visit I definitely knew I wanted to come to Connecticut. One of the big keys was Coach Auriemma. Obviously, he was a good coach. I could tell that by his record and the way practice went. As a person he is very funny and has a great personality. And that is what I was looking for in a coach off the court. Someone who I could go in and see them in their office and sit down and talk. They hadn't been to the Final Four yet, but I didn't care. The people here are what drove me. They could have had a losing record, and I probably still would have come here just because I felt so good about the people."

As the early signing period approached, Vincent urged Lobo to schedule a press conference to announce her choice. She was hesitant. "I'm afraid no one will come," she joked.

On the first day for commitments, Auriemma called Dailey into his office. Lobo was on the phone. "She started off saying, 'Coach, I really want to thank you . . . ,' and when they start off that way you think, oh God, they're going somewhere else," Dailey says. "And then she said, 'I've decided to come to Connecticut.' "

Lobo was a major key in the continuing development of UConn women's basketball. For the first time, the program had competed on the national level for a top player and been successful. The landing of Lobo, coupled with the team's first Final Four appearance five months later, had UConn knocking at the penthouse door.

But Lobo would ultimately serve a purpose well beyond that of blue-chip attention getter. On the court, she would set a tone with her hard work and unselfish play. Off the court, she would become perhaps the single greatest ambassador not only for UConn women's basketball but for women's basketball in general.

"I guess I have to see myself as a role model because a parent may come up and say thanks for being such a great role model or because of the way a little kid might look at you," Lobo says. "I don't mind it at all. I've always lived a certain way and will continue to do so. And not because someone is telling me I'm a role model. Well, I'm not a role model, that's just the way I am. If someone can take something positive from that, then that is great. But no one can choose whether they are going to be a role model. Some people are just going to look at them in that way or they are not. So it's something I accept and it's not something I mind."

One of the major things that had parents dragging kids by the psyche to Lobo's side was her academic achievements. In the eighth grade, Lobo had done poorly on a test and was told by her mother that if her grades slipped there would be no more basketball. Lobo got the message. She was salutatorian of her high school graduating class, a member of the National Honor Society, and a Massachusetts Academic All-Star.

As a political science major at the University of Connecticut, Lobo made the dean's list every semester and had a 3.7 overall grade point average, which included a perfect 4.0 the first semester of her senior year. In addition to being voted the best women's college basketball player in the country her senior year, Lobo was also selected as the game's top student. Included among her academic honors were GTE/CoSIDA National Academic All-American of the Year, GTE/CoSIDA First Team Academic All-American, U.S.B.W.A. Women's Basketball Scholar-Athlete of the Year, Big East Women's Basketball Scholar-Athlete of the Year, Big East Academic All-Star Team, and UConn Club Outstanding Senior Scholar Athlete. She was also inducted into the Phi Beta Kappa National Honor Society and was a Rhodes scholar nominee.

Among the courses Lobo took her senior year was a class in English literature taught by Samuel F. Pickering, Jr., who was the model for the eccentric teacher played by Robin Williams in *Dead Poets Society.*

"I look around the classroom," Pickering told one interviewer, "and pick out the people who have sunlight shining from their eyes. Rebecca is one of them. She never misses a class. She's a throwback to what we all dream about as the ultimate student athlete. And there are so few of them. I'm against big-time college athletics, and Rebecca is the sort of person who makes you rethink that."

"My self-discipline definitely comes from my parents," Lobo says. "They have always let me know that if you have committed yourself to doing something that you not only are going to do it, but you are going to do it as well as you can and are going to prepare yourself as well as you can. I've always looked at things and figured out what I wanted to get out of them and then did what I could to get them. At the time, I didn't realize I was being goal-oriented, but looking back I guess I really was. I just think that if it's possible for you to do something, I think you should be able to do it. I'm pretty laid back until it comes time to reach a goal. If I want to do something, I want to do it well, not just do it. I don't think there is any point in that."

Given all that she has accomplished, given the star treatment she has received from the time she was in grade school, it would be easy for Lobo to have become stuck on herself, to become one of those aloof, unapproachable, temperamental types that dominate sports these days. She is the direct opposite. Rebecca Lobo the person is as impressive as Rebecca Lobo the athlete and Rebecca Lobo the student.

She is unfailingly polite to everyone, sensitive, down-to-earth, accommodating, and generous with her time to a fault. She never leaves games until the last kid is greeted, the last autograph signed. She visits schools and attends charity functions and answers her bags of fan mail personally. She is extremely popular with her teammates, opponents, fellow students, and anybody who knows her personally. She is one of those people about whom no one has a bad word to say. She is, in short, too good to be true, but she is.

For most women players, their last game is the last time anyone hears about them. But for Lobo the National Championship and 35-0 were just the beginning.

In the weeks after the championship game, Lobo appeared as a guest on "Late Night with David Letterman" and "Regis and Kathie Lee" and shot a round with Harry Smith on "CBS This Morning."

She signed an endorsement deal with Spaulding and a multiyear deal with Reebok, which could make her one of the most prominent female athletes in the country, particularly among preteen and teenage girls. "We see Rebecca as becoming one of our lead female icons," said a Reebok executive. "We want Rebecca to communicate to young girls the benefit of sports."

In mid-May, Lobo traveled to Colorado to try out for the Olympic team and was one of eleven players selected. She will tour with the team for a year and then play in the 1996 Summer Olympic Games in Atlanta. After that, she may go to Europe and play in a women's professional league.

Because she missed the team's White House visit in May, Lobo was extended an invitation to run with President Clinton in June. She was accompanied by her brother, Jason. "I was just sitting there waiting in a room with a couple of people and he came down without anyone around him in his jogging clothes and came over yawning," Lobo recalls. "He seemed like a normal human being that just got out of bed and was about to go for a jog. He just started talking to us and at first you are kind of guarded about what you are going to say, but then he was joking around and he made me feel real comfortable. It was almost like I had to hit myself a couple of times and say, this is the President of the United States."

In between visiting with the President and appearing on

network television and trying out for and touring with the Olympic team and signing endorsement deals, Lobo also made several paid appearances at a local department store. She was surprised by the reaction she received, which was still strong three months after the Tennessee game. "When I went to the first store I was surprised," Lobo says, "but I just thought it was the first chance people had had to see me. They were so nice. They came up and said congratulations and had nice stories to tell that really made you feel good about yourself and about what you have done. If I hadn't gone out and done these things, I wouldn't have understood how winning the championship affected other people's lives. It's a good way to appreciate that. But I still don't understand it, I mean, my mom wouldn't wait in line to see me, so I don't know why these other people are."

Although she has always received a fair amount of attention, Lobo admits to having some difficulty adjusting to being a full-blown celebrity. "Sometimes it can be hard," she says, "because your life changes in ways that you never expected it to. I have to do things differently now than in the past. I just can't go to a mall now and go shopping. So in some respects it's hard because you have less of yourself, less time for yourself. But on the other hand, there are good things about it. Just the fact that people appreciate what you have done is always very nice. But I've struggled with it a little bit.

"People do treat me differently now, not because I have changed as a person, but because I have changed as a basketball player and because of what my team has done on the basketball court. When you step off the basketball court you are still the same person, even though you are not the same player. You have to understand that they are not treating you any better because you have all of a sudden done something as a person that made you deserve this."

Although Lobo has seen UConn women's basketball grow and prosper during her watch, she says the basic components of the program she helped elevate have remained essentially unchanged. "I think the work ethic is the same from the first day I got here to the day before the National Championship game," she says. "I think Coach is the same as when I was a freshman. He won't accept anything other than everyone trying their best. Those are the types of players he recruits, that is the type of program he runs."

Geno Auriemma

The perfectionist, having attained the unattainable, perfection, is sitting in his office in the aftermath of 35-0 dreading the future. He knows his story should end right here, right now, that he should ride into the sunset on the wings of unparalleled success and not look back. He knows that the chances of ever again achieving on such a lofty plane are remote. And he knows that expectations will be such from here on out that merely being good, or even great for that matter, will not be enough. Geno Auriemma knows he has created a monster, one he knows he must now control or be devoured by.

"Don't think I haven't thought about walking away," he is saying from a soft chair in a comfortable office decorated in the statuary of accomplishment. "Life from here on in is going to be nothing but misery. It's like when I hit that five iron a hundred and eighty-five yards a foot from the pin. From then on, every other five iron will not be good enough unless it goes in. Everything I do from here on in I will compare to this.

"I don't know how I'm going to deal with it. That is the lesson to be learned. That is the true test. How am I going to deal with falling short of thirty-five and O and the National Championship? I have to figure out what my approach is going to be with my players, my family, kids. I want to make sure everyone doesn't get sucked in by all of this and destroyed by it all.

"You know, people leave you alone when you are trying to build something. They don't bother you. Then they look up at you and say, wow, look what you did. And then they all want to drag you away from that, ask you to be this, be that, do this. And a year goes by and you look up and say, damn, we're not where we were last year. And now those same people are saying, see, you couldn't handle success. In today's world it's hard to repeat. It's hard to do it again and again. Why? People won't let you alone. That, I think, is the real hurdle we have to overcome. I don't want my players to become celebrities. They're students and then basketball players. But everyone wants them to be something else now."

Auriemma, a worrier by nature and profession, is also concerned about the effect the season of unbridled success will have on those who follow the team. Fan support has always been an important element for the UConn women. Even when the numbers weren't there, the personal attachment, win or lose, was. But what now? Will they have grown so accustomed to success that they can only find fulfillment now in triumph? Will their love become conditional? Will they be there in the foul weather as they had been in the fair?

"It's like I tell my players," Auriemma says, "your strength can also become your weakness if you are not careful. What makes you a good player, you're intense, work hard. What happens if you are too intense, never know when to back off. Two days after we win the National Championship Jen Rizzotti's in here for three hours playing three on three. Jen, relax. Working hard is a strength she has that makes her a great player, but she has to be careful.

"A strength that our fans have is that they are passionate about winning, about being the best. But they have to be careful and not let that become a weakness. There is another side to that. Do you expect us to be striving to reach that level every day? Yeah, because we do too. But you must understand that there are pitfalls along the way. Only one team gets there. What about the other 301 Division One schools? Expect us to try and be there, but if your expectation is I'm not going to be happy unless we win the National Championship, then you are going to spend more unhappy days than happy days.

"I mean, this isn't anything different than what I worry about with my team. Pam Webber thinks she works harder than any basketball player in America. Guess what? She does. But does that mean she should have a National Championship ring? In my mind, yeah. What if she never gets one, she's going to think, man, I wanted that so bad, why didn't I get it? Well, not everybody gets one. But not everyone has a chance to go for the ride. So you made a right turn before you got there, it still was a great ride. You have to have passion for your team, love your team, cry when we lose, cry when we win. But you have to love us every single day. When we lose, you've got to wake up the next morning and say, we're going to get them today, who's next, we're going to kick their butt.

"I have to set our level of expectation. I can't let people set it for me. We've given everyone a chance to drink from the cup. If we are extremely fortunate, maybe we'll get another chance. But if we don't, you have to remember what it tasted like. There are a lot of people who have only had the bad taste, never had the good taste. A lot of people say to me, Geno, you can do it again next year. Hey, it's only been done once in Connecticut history, and now you expect us to do it twice in a row?"

Despite the ongoing angst, the fear of the future, the burden of success, Geno Auriemma is content. He has family, friends, financial security, and fame. He is, at age forty, at the top of his profession. He is, in his eleventh year, the patriarch of a program that is admired nationally. He is, at once, not only living the American dream but the embodiment of it.

Auriemma's standard one-liner when asked about his childhood immigration is that his mother put him on a boat bound for America and told him, "Go win the National Championship." It didn't quite happen that way.

Luigi (Geno) Auriemma arrived in the United States at age seven from the tiny mountain village of Montella in southern Italy. His father had come over the previous year to find a better life, leaving his three children and wife behind. Donato Auriemma found work in a steel mill, and the family joined him a year later. They settled in Norristown, Pennsylvania, a suburb of Philadelphia that also produced Dodgers manager Tommy Lasorda. The year was 1961.

Geno Auriemma entered second grade at the local Catholic grammar school wearing homemade clothes and not speaking a word of English. By the end of the school year, he had mastered his new language well enough to be promoted and also to become the family spokesman. He took his mother shopping, made the rounds with her once a month to pay the bills, and even signed his own report cards.

In Italy, Auriemma had walked two miles to play soccer, but in America he fell in love with baseball, a game he played whenever possible at the local playground. "Somebody once asked me what I wanted to be when I grew up," Auriemma says. "What would be the epitome of happiness for you? And I said I wished I could be eleven years old. Because when I was eleven years old, you couldn't get any better than that."

At Bishop Kendrick High School, Auriemma began playing basketball, making the team as a backup point guard. Basketball coach Buddy Gardler remembers the 5-foot-10, 155-pound Auriemma as someone who "wasn't scaring anyone with his talent." Auriemma spent most of his time on the bench but didn't complain. He was happy to be a member of the team and he admired Gardler greatly.

Following his graduation from high school, Auriemma enrolled at Montgomery County Community College, where he teamed up at guard with Jim Foster, now the women's basketball coach at Vanderbilt. From Montgomery, Auriemma transferred to West Chester University, where he majored in political science.

"One of my first role models was my high school basketball

coach," Auriemma says. "I thought teaching history and coaching high school basketball would be kind of a neat thing to do. Until I found out how much he made and said, whoa, that's not going to work out."

As a student, Auriemma became fascinated with the framers of the constitution, figures such as Jefferson, Franklin, and Madison. He would spend hours at the college library, where he worked part-time, reading the Federalist Papers and studying the Revolutionary War. He was also vice president of the law club. "If I had been as disciplined as Rebecca Lobo or Pam Webber, I wouldn't be here right now," Auriemma says. "I'd be an attorney someplace. I loved it, loved reading all about it. But I didn't have what it takes to go through the process. My wife always tells me I should be a lawyer because I can argue both sides in about thirty seconds."

Kathy Osler met Geno Auriemma when they were freshmen at Montgomery. He played basketball; she was a cheerleader, a role she says hasn't changed that much over the years. The two dated throughout college and beyond, finally getting married in 1978 after a six-year courtship. The couple now have three children, Jenna, eleven; Alysa, nine; and Michael, six.

When the newlyweds walked out of the church in 1978, they were virtually penniless, a lifestyle they maintained over the first several years of their marriage. Auriemma's first job was as an assistant to his former teammate, Foster, who was the head women's coach at St. Joseph's University in Philadelphia. The pay was $1,000. To pay the bills, Auriemma worked in the steel mills, poured drinks, taught gym classes, even stocked shelves in a grocery store.

In 1981, he got his first break when he was hired as an assistant by Debbie Ryan at Virginia. In his first two years, Auriemma recruited six high school All-Americans, and in his third year, Virginia went 24-8 and won the Atlantic Coast Conference regular-season title. By the time the 1984–85 season rolled around, Auriemma was looking to strike out on his own, and if the truth be told, Ryan was not opposed to his moving on. In the summer of 1985, Auriemma, the man Ryan describes as being "a supremely confident human being," was hired by the University of Connecticut.

The rest, as they say, is history:

One day you're this young guy schmoozing a search committee and trying to get your first head coaching job. And the next you're the Naismith National Coach of the Year, the Associated Press National Coach of the Year, the United States Basketball Writers Association National Coach of the Year, the College Sports Magazine National Coach of the Year, the Big East Conference Coach of the Year.

One day you're 9-19 and laying carpet in the locker room yourself and fighting to get a push-button phone for your office. And the next you're 35-0, and National Champions, and the coach of the best college women's basketball team ever.

One day you're an immigrant kid in homemade clothes lugging all your family's belongings to a new country, a new culture. And the next you're wearing an expensive suit and standing in the East Room of the White House, and the President of the United States is standing at a podium telling the world that your team "did more to make the rest of America appreciate women's basketball than any team that has ever played."

"We're standing there waiting for the President to come out," Auriemma says, "and Lew Perkins [UConn athletic director] is standing next to me, kidding me, saying, 'Just remember: Norristown, Pennsylvania, Italian kid from Norristown, Pennsylvania.'

"There were only three times during the year when I didn't know what to say, how to act. The first is after we won the National Championship and people asked me, 'How does it feel?' How do I know? I have no idea. I can't answer that question. I wish I could be eloquent with you, but I can't. What does it feel like to be thirty-five and O, National Champions? I have no idea.

"The second time is when I got the Naismith award. I'm getting the Naismith award. I'm National Coach of the Year, not just anybody's National Coach of the Year, Naismith's. What am I supposed to say? I don't know what to say."

The third time Auriemma found himself muzzled by the moment was at the White House. When he had received the call from President Clinton in the locker room in Minneapolis, Auriemma had been relatively unimpressed. He viewed the guy on the other end of the line more as Bill Clinton than as Mr. President.

A month later, on the way to Washington, he continued to be underwhelmed, thinking in typically cocky fashion, "White House, hey, what's the big deal, we've been lots of places." Perhaps, because he had assimilated the culture so well, he never saw his White House visit as the defining scene in a classic rags-to-riches story. His father, however, had immediately viewed the occasion in terms of the American dream.

"When my father heard we were going to the White House, he wanted to know if he could come with us," Auriemma says. "He told me, 'I'm the kind of guy the President should want to meet.' I said what are you talking about? He said, 'Look at me, I'm what America is supposed to be. I'm the guy who got an opportunity. My kids were brought up here. Lived a pretty good life here. That never would have happened where we used to live in Italy. I should get a chance to meet him.' "

Auriemma's indifference vanished the minute the occupant of the Oval Office appeared. "Suddenly I'm standing face to face with the guy and I have to say something," Auriemma says. "I don't know if it's the office or what, but when you're around the guy for about thirty seconds, you feel like he is looking right through you. He had just come out of that Bosnia meeting about one of our planes being shot down. But the way he was talking to us, you would have thought he had been up all night thinking about women's basketball. And then you have to stand up at the podium and talk while he is standing behind you. I have no idea what I said, if it even made any sense or not.

"When he said that we had done more for women's basketball, no one wrote that for him. When he talked to me the first time in the locker room he said things about people on our team that he couldn't have known unless he had caught a couple of games on TV. And what he said about us and women's basketball was absolutely right. Women's basketball in this country will never be the same."

One might assume the afterglow of such accomplishment, such recognition, would prompt reflection. But that was not the case for Auriemma. "Unless someone asks me about the beginning, I never put then and now together," he says. "It's like that was one world and this is another. I don't even go over to the Field House because I know I'll look around and go, holy jeez. Maybe I should go over just to remind myself. But it just seems so far back, so long ago, so far removed.

"I know how all this happened, but I can't describe it. You go to work every morning, so does every other coach. You watch game films, so does every other coach. You go to practice. You go recruiting. You don't do anything different than anybody else. So why do some people win all the time? In some ways, we're fortunate. But it's not just luck. We share some things that are just vital to winning, and if you don't have them, then it doesn't matter how hard you work. Vince Lombardi said the difference between a good coach and a great coach is that a great coach knows when it looks right. Some guys never know what it's supposed to look like. They fool themselves. That looks good, we got it. No they don't. Other guys, their team will play really good, but they're pissed off. Why? Because something really didn't look right. That night after we beat Tennessee, won the National Championship, I pop the tape in, we're all sitting around watching, and five plays into the game I hit the pause button: Jesus Christ, what happened there? Jen and a couple of other guys turned around and threw stuff at me. Said shut up, we won the game. But for me, it's always there."

On the bus ride from the airport to Gampel Pavilion for the postchampionship reception, Auriemma watched the excitement inside the bus and wondered about the future. What would his life be like now? How would everything he had accomplished affect his family, his relationships, his program? "I've created a whole new world," he thought, "and now I have to live in it."

Recruiting

What makes a great coach? Great players. What makes an elite program? Elite players. "Sometimes people will say, even if you don't have the players, you can outcoach the other team," Calhoun says. "Well, you aren't going to outcoach the Derrick Colemans and the Alonzo Mournings. That kind of talent is going to win out over the long term."

Nothing that either the UConn men or women have been able to accomplish in the past ten years would have been even remotely possible without the caliber of student athletes the programs have been able to attract. How you find these people, how you evaluate them, how you get them to come to your institution is a mini-industry within a big-time business. In days of yore, kids were lured with promises of clothes and cash and even automobiles. The joke about one big-time coach who had a penchant for recruiting junior college players was that he preferred such kids because their cars were already paid for.

In today's world of tight restrictions and strict enforcement, everybody pretty much operates under the same rules while at the same time playing different games. Every program has its system for identifying, courting, and signing players. The process is arduous, expensive, time-consuming, intense, pressure-filled, sophisticated, and very competitive.

When Calhoun walked into Howie Dickenman's office in the spring of 1986, he noticed a group photo of four current players on the assistant coach's wall. Dickenman had been advised that he would be smart to start looking for another job after Dom Perno resigned, but he had declined. If the new coach didn't want to hire him, well, that was okay with Dickenman. But he wasn't going to quit on the kids he had recruited into the program, the kids in the photo on his wall. That kind of loyalty impressed Calhoun, and within ten minutes of accepting the job as head coach, he says he hired Howie Dickenman.

"Nobody, absolutely nobody out there, compares to Howie," Calhoun says ten years later. "He is the best. I trust my recruiting life to him. Given the competition he faces, one hundred schools, given our tradition or lack thereof, he consistently gets me into position to do what I do best, which is sit down with Mom and Dad."

While Dickenman was Calhoun's first official decision, Geno Auriemma was talking about hiring Chris Dailey even before he had the job. Why? Because the person in charge of recruiting is a new coach's most important decision. Why? Because he had recruited against Dailey when he was an assistant at Virginia, and he knew how good she was at not only sizing up talent but judging character.

"They bicker like kids," says Meghan Pattyson, who has played under and coached alongside Dailey and Auriemma. "But they are a tremendous combination. Geno likes to do the PR stuff, he's smooth. Chris, on the other hand, goes out and pounds the trails. She finds the kids, coordinates all the recruiting. She also handles the administrative stuff, basically runs the office. Geno has a lot of trust in Chris, primarily because they have been together for so long. When you think about the ideal assistant, she is it, especially for him."

"We will start off recruiting a hundred and fifty to two hundred players for next season, and we want to maybe sign four," Dickenman says. "We're trying to go on a two percent success rate. That's low, but those are the numbers we deal with. Recruiting is a tough business. It's a business where your success is dependent on seventeen-year-old kids. They affect your ride home, how you sleep, how you eat, your mental attitude. There's a lot of pressure to get the players. As good a coach as Jim Calhoun is, if he doesn't have the players, he isn't going to win."

Dickenman, who was born in Norwich, Connecticut, on November 10, 1946, earned All-American honors at Central Connecticut State University in the late sixties, surpassing the one thousand mark in both points and rebounds. He joined UConn under Perno in 1982 following four years as an assistant at Canisius. In 1994, he was named associate head coach by Calhoun as a reward for his "loyalty, hard work, dedication to a cause, and relentless pursuit of excellence."

"A recruiter has to be a good guy. You have to make yourself a popular guy. You may not like some of the things people tell you, but you have to ride those waves," Dickenman says. "The other thing is you have to have a good reputation. You have to be honest. You can't promise things you can't deliver."

When Dickenman recruited during the Perno era, UConn was considered a regional program, even though it competed in the Big East Conference. Thus, it recruited regionally. This resulted in a huge disadvantage for the program because conference opponents such as Georgetown, Syracuse, and St. John's played a national schedule and, as a result, recruited nationally.

"I remember when we got Tim Coles out of Baltimore [1983] and everybody was amazed," Dickenman says. "They were saying, 'Wow, Connecticut is really branching out.' Now if we got someone from Baltimore, it would be one of the closest places.

"When Jim came aboard, we decided to go out and sell the league. We didn't worry about barriers or boundaries. The Big East was a premiere league. The television exposure was second to none, and kids always envision themselves on TV. Big East basketball was a great advertisement, even if Connecticut wasn't one of the top teams at the time."

"We used the Carrier Dome, Derrick Coleman, Alonzo Mourning, all the great stars of the Big East to recruit for us," Calhoun says. "We became more successful once we got on TV ourselves, but going national was by design. It didn't just happen."

While the Big East and its television package was a definite

plus, UConn still had obstacles of its own making to overcome in the beginning.

"I remember recruiting this kid, and the day he is supposed
to visit we're practicing in the Field House and it was rain-
ing," Dickenman says. "Our graduate assistant at the time
had to go pick the kid up at the airport. Before he left I told
him, I don't care how you bring him, New Haven, Massachusetts, just don't get him here while we are practicing. I want
practice to be over when he comes. Some media were there
that day, and they counted twenty-one towels we had on the
floor because of leaks in the roof. For us to say this is where
you are going to play but don't worry about the twenty-one
towels because all that rain will be ice in the wintertime would
have been ridiculous. The kid had visited Purdue before us,
and I'm walking him back to the plane and he promises me he
wasn't going to sign early. Two days later, he signed with
Purdue. We went to play Purdue a couple of years later. Looking at their facilities, I said, man, if I had the choice I would
have gone to Purdue."

While Gampel Pavilion was a boost in terms of recruiting, it
was only a factor. Prior to its opening in January of 1990,
such players as Clifford Robinson, Phil Gamble, Tate George,
Chris Smith, Murray Williams, Nadav Henefeld, Scott Burrell,
and Rod Sellers had all been successfully convinced Storrs was
the place for them.

Today, the UConn men are the most geographically diverse
team in the country. The thirteen members of the 1994–95
team hailed from ten different states, including Arizona, California, Connecticut, Florida, Georgia, Louisiana, South Caro-

lina, Texas, Utah, and Washington. In addition, there were two players from Israel.

"When I used to call kids ten years ago, I would tell them I was from the University of Connecticut in the Big East Conference," Dickenman says. "I don't have to do that anymore. Because of television, a kid, say, on the West Coast is just getting home from practice at five P.M. when we are playing a game on ESPN. They see the Big East Conference and Connecticut all the time now."

Despite the program's national flavor and the team's success in the nineties, there remain certain locales where Connecticut enjoys little if any recruiting success.

"To this day we can't get a kid out of New York City," Calhoun says. "We don't have the AAU contacts there, nor do I want to have them. The price is too high to pay. I don't want to become involved with some of those guys who deal with agents."

Dickenman says they also usually avoid going after players in Big Ten country and kids that certain schools such as North Carolina, Duke, or Kentucky may be hot to trot for: "If we're competing for a kid and Duke wants him, we're probably not going to beat Duke. We can try, but a key thing in recruiting is to know when to fold 'em and when to hold 'em. You don't want to spin your wheels.

"In recruiting, you have to press the right button. You have to know who is the right person. Every kid will tell you, I'm making the decisions. You ask the parents, coach, they'll tell you he's going to make up his own mind. But I doubt if any seventeen-year-old makes a decision without asking someone, without leaning on someone. So you have to find that person. It might be the parents, coach, guidance counselor.

"In Cliff Robinson's case, it was his math teacher. We knew that and catered to him. Ironically, his name was Bill Russell.

"With Chris Smith, it was the athletic director at Kolbe Cathedral. When we first went down to Bridgeport to see Chris, his family was not very familiar with the University of Connecticut. They did not even know where we were. We determined the key person to be the athletic director. She ended up working with us. She knew the best place for Chris was Connecticut because of what he could do for us and what we could do for him."

After identifying recruits, Dickenman keeps track of them through a stack of file cards. Each card contains vital statistics about the recruit: height, weight, position, stats. As the recruiting process goes on, other information, such as key contact and personal quirks, is added. As recruits are eliminated, Dickenman's stack of index cards dwindles down to a precious few.

The bulk of the recruiting process centers around making and keeping the player aware of your interest. Because contact with players is limited, how a program keeps itself in the forefront of a player's mind is where recruiting becomes an art form.

"When you go to see kids play you usually can't talk to them, but you want them to know you are there," Dickenman says. "So you have to strategically position yourself. Say you go to a tournament in Las Vegas with eighty teams there and you're watching a number of kids. Every coach there is wearing a shirt with the name of his school on it.

You're a walking billboard, a walking advertisement. If you are really into recruiting a certain player, maybe during warm-ups you get into a corner near where he is shooting layups so that he sees you. Or maybe you hang around the water fountain. Or if you know he will be leaving the building a certain way, you casually go hang around outside there.

"Because you can't talk to the kid, maybe you give your card to his coach with a little note on it: 'Terry, really enjoyed watching you play. Good Luck.' Some people will write a note and give it to the coach, who ends up walking out with five or six letters in his hand. The reason I don't do that is I want to be different. I'm going to maybe call the hotel where the player is staying, get his voice mail: 'Hi, Terry, Coach Dickenman, thought you played real well. Good luck in tomorrow's game at four P.M.' So the kid comes back and gets voice mail from Connecticut.

"Something we just started doing is using portable phones. I'll be watching a game, and from the stands I'll call the kid's parents at their home: 'Hi, this is Coach Dickenman from Connecticut. I'm watching your son play right now, he has sixteen points at the half. The team is playing well, winning.' Maybe after the game, the kid calls home and says we won. And the parents say I know. Well, how do you know? Coach Dickenman from Connecticut called.'"

Another device used to express interest is mail. In a busy week during the height of the recruiting process, each of the 150 to 200 players on the recruiting list may get as many as five pieces of mail from UConn. Usually, the mailing includes a piece of information about the university or the program or a newspaper story that casts a favorable light. With every piece of mail there is a brief note, two or three lines at the most, which is always signed. For those identified as "special recruits" by UConn, personal, handwritten notes are often included. "High school coaches have told me that the most mail kids get is from the University of Connecticut," Dickenman says. "That's not because we are out working other places. It's just that with the media following we get, we have the luxury of sending a lot of articles."

During periods when phone contact is allowed, one call per week, Dickenman, Calhoun, and the other coaches all make calls. The conversations are generally short, the point, again, to plant the seed, reinforce the perception of interest. If the player doesn't happen to be home, a short message is left on the answering machine.

Besides the standard approaches, sometimes a little innovation is called for. Such was the case with Scott Burrell, a tremendously gifted athlete who was ultimately drafted in the first round by the Charlotte Hornets of the NBA. Although Burrell was from the state and his brother was a member of the UConn football team, he was not recruited until late in the game because basketball was not his primary interest. As a football player, Burrell was good enough to be sought by the University of Notre Dame. And as a pitcher with a ninety-plus-miles-per-hour fastball, he was signed by Toronto. It wasn't until Burrell went to a basketball camp before his senior year and came back rated in the blue-chipper stratosphere that the chase began.

"I remember driving down to his house twice on Friday afternoons after articles were written on why Scott Burrell should attend UConn," Dickenman says. "I took the newspaper and stuck it under the mat on his front porch. Then I drove down the street and called him up: 'Scotty, check the newspaper I just delivered to your house.' "

Sometimes recruiting comes down to luck, which was the case with Ray Allen. Connecticut was only getting a lukewarm response from Allen during the fall early recruiting period. Dickenman was scheduled to fly to Louisiana to talk to Kirk King, another recruit, on the first day the rules allowed coaches to approach players. Weather grounded the flight in Tennessee, however, so at the last minute Dickenman decided to fly to Columbia, South Carolina, and see if he could talk to Allen.

"So I go to Ray's high school, unannounced, and the coach gets him. We sit down, and I can see we are connecting. We have eye-to-eye contact for a half hour, good vibes. He is very appreciative that we are the first ones down to see him. I said, well, the reason we are here to see you first, Ray, is because you are special. I didn't tell him I was really supposed to be seeing Kirk King. When Ray later decided to come to Connecticut, he said what had really impressed him was that we were the first ones down to see him. And I wasn't even supposed to be there."

If Dickenman has done his job, a visit to the player's home will be arranged for Calhoun. These visits are allowed over a three-week period in September. Scheduling and maximizing the allotted time is very important. Although a school is allowed to have two coaches on the road at the same time during this span, Calhoun usually goes out alone. It is more difficult on him, but it is more efficient because it lets Dickenman or another assistant be somewhere else at the same time. So twice as much can be accomplished.

"All the assistant does if there are two of you is sit there," Dickenman says. "He hears the same stories, laughs at the same jokes. If I go with Jim my job is to pet the dog, say the cookies are great. It's nice for Jim to have the company, but I can be doing something better somewhere else. Another advantage is Jim can say the reason I'm here alone is because you are going to play for me. You know Coach Dickenman, talked to him on the phone. I wanted to give you a chance to meet me, for us to get to know each other."

The in-home sales pitch has some staples, such as developing the player as a person and graduation rates, but the message varies. Chris Smith was told that if he came to Storrs, UConn would get on CBS. Now the program is preaching National Championship and development as a player. "We only had two players in the history of the school who were McDonald's All-Americans, the very elite," Dickenman says. "They were Corny Thompson and Donyell Marshall. But if you look at the NBA you see Clifford Robinson, Tate George, Scott Burrell, Chris Smith, Donny Marshall, probably Travis Knight, definitely Ray Allen. We tell recruits that we strive to develop players to their fullest. And just look at players in the NBA. See what a good job we've done?"

Engaging in negative recruiting, rival programs will often seek to use the location of the UConn campus in rural Storrs as a means of dissuading players who come mainly from cities. UConn is the only Big East school that is not located in or near an urban center. "I had a kid come one time, and I showed him the Civic Center in Hartford and then drove to campus," Dickenman says. "I always drive a little faster when I do this so the distance seems shorter. I get to campus, twenty-two miles, and the kid says, 'I didn't realize it was so close. Another coach told me you needed a helicopter to get from Hartford to the campus.' "

Calhoun has even turned this potential negative into a positive, emphasizing the safety the rural location affords. "I tell them it's a city you are going to," Calhoun says, "but it is a protected city. When someone drives over that hill on Route 195, I tell Mom and Dad, I'm going to know who it is."

Besides giving a coach limited access to a player's home, recruiting rules also allow a school to provide a player with an expenses-paid visit to its campus. While the home visit is probably more important in terms of swaying parents, the campus visit plays a larger role in the player's ultimate decision. This, after all, is the community in which he will play, live, learn, socialize, grow. When all the wining and dining and selling are over, a player usually picks the institution where he feels most comfortable.

At the same time a player is checking out UConn, Calhoun and company are using the visit to evaluate the player. Particularly important is what kind of person the player is and how, or if, he will fit in. Although the UConn men's and women's programs are worlds apart in many ways, one thing they do have in common is the type of athletes they recruit. Each tends to attract kids who are not only good players but good people, solid citizens who are responsible and hardworking and have established values. "I had someone once tell me that the reason we have good kids in our program is because 'a shithead wouldn't put up with you,' " Calhoun says. "He was probably right."

"If a kid is a headache in high school, chances are pretty good he is going to be the same way in college and probably right into the NBA," Dickenman says. "We do a very thorough job. When a kid visits here, we make a point of asking the player who hosted him, what do you think? Does he fit in with us? There have been three players in my experience here at Connecticut where the people hosting a kid said, 'Coach, I'm not sure this would be the right school for him.' All three of those players went to other Big East schools, and all three had problems."

"I won't decide based just on what the kids think," Calhoun says. "You create a family atmosphere, and the kids get to be like brothers. When new guys come aboard there is resentment from the older guys, not because they don't like them but because the younger guys are taking playing time away from their brothers. They wouldn't intentionally hurt the program, but if they weren't crazy about the guy, they might make it worse. On the other hand, if I have a kid I really trust come to me and say you're going to have a tough time with this guy. . . .

"You have to look around you and see where you are. We had this kid from Bridgeport come in, good player, but when he came here he had a toothpick in his mouth. I said when you go meet some people today, it might be a good idea to take the toothpick out. It doesn't bother me a bit, but certain people might get a wrong connotation, might make certain value judgments without you even opening your mouth. He took it out, but Sunday when he left, he had the toothpick back in his mouth. It may seem like a small thing, but I knew this kid would have a tough time at UConn.

"I'm going to push kids as hard as I can. Ray Allen understands that. Cliff Robinson tried to understand, and now that he makes three million a year, he really understands. You need a certain kind of kid who can understand what you are trying to do. If I'm going face-to-face with you, well, it's tough. So you need certain kinds of kids. We generally prefer kids from stable home environments so we can call parents and talk to them, explain what we are trying to do, keep them informed. Ours is a very family-oriented atmosphere. But will I sometimes take kids who are good players but could go either way, kids that are going to be more followers than leaders, kids that hopefully are going to be influenced by the group? Yes."

The UConn women, in comparison, place an extremely high premium on how a recruit fits into the team fabric. Attracting and blending the right kinds of kids is at the very core of Auriemma's coaching philosophy. "In recruiting, a five is a superstar, a Rebecca Lobo coming out of high school," Auriemma says. "I would take a kid who is a four if I thought she had all the intangibles it takes for winning over a kid who is a five, who is missing those things. I think in the long run we are going to win more games because of it."

What is unique about Auriemma's approach to recruiting is that he consciously, actively pursues chemistry, as opposed to most coaches, who simply go after the best players and then hope that the group they finally assemble will come together as a team. "The compromise is made when you have a kid with great ability who has no regard for anybody else," Auriemma says. "The coach tells himself, I'm such a good coach, I'm such a great psychologist, that I can take any kids and make them what I want them to be. Well, that ain't going to happen. That's an ego thing.

"Chemistry is the ingredient present in most great teams. Where does that come from? It comes from people who have chemistry as people. People who have chemistry are people who take the time to listen to what you have to say. They're not into themselves, their egos are intact, they are a giving, sacrificing kind of person. That is the kind of person who will pass you the ball when you are wide-open. Kids that are unselfish to begin with are going to play unselfishly. Think of some of the players I've had:

"Pam Webber wasn't recruited by schools in the Top Ten, Top Twenty. But you take a kid like her. Why? Well, in four years here she never missed a practice, never missed a workout, never missed a game. How much does that contribute to winning? Immensely.

"Wendy Davis grows up forty-five minutes from Penn State, but they don't bat an eyelash at her. Too slow, not tall enough, not quick enough. She comes here and is All Big East, second leading scorer in the history of the program. She makes every single jump shot. Why? Because she has to. So how did you know she would be good? Well, she's a straight-A student. Everyone you talk to says she would do anything to contribute to family, friends, school. That tells you she just wants to win games, that she is not about how many shots she gets, how many points she scores."

In Lobo, Auriemma found his perfect recruit, a six-foot-four walking well of chemistry: great student, nice person, no ego, unselfish to a fault, and an undisputed five.

"Watch Rebecca Lobo play sometime," Auriemma says. "She's the first kid off the bench when someone comes off the court, hands them a towel, pats them on the butt. She throws a pass to a kid and it goes through her hands, she runs up the floor, pats her on the back, don't worry about it. That's exactly what superstars do, right? Of course not, they make faces, get pissed off. When you get a kid that *doesn't* do that, well. . . ."

The recruiting process begins with Dailey, who usually makes the initial contact. In some cases, interest in a player can end after a single phone call. "There are times when I'll have a conversation with a kid on the phone and I know right away that she will never have a conversation with Geno," Dailey says. "I'm sure that I have been wrong, but I think I'm pretty much on target once I get a feel for a kid. Sometimes you know right away that a kid, no matter how good they are, won't be involved in our program."

Auriemma is also adept at quickly getting a read on a recruit. "Geno knows people very, very well," Pattyson says. "He is tremendous at talking to a kid, even one time, and knowing if it's his type of kid or not."

When Dailey goes to summer camps to see players in action, much of the emphasis is on character, personality. "We have always just gone by a kind of a feel," Dailey says. "You go to camps and there are coaches that write down everything a kid does. We've developed a system in which I feel the more I have to write down about a kid, the less chance she will fit in. We kind of go with gut reaction on a lot of things."

As a high school player, UConn All-American Jen Rizzotti had a reputation as a fierce competitor. Dailey remembers watching a game in which play had to be stopped because of water on the floor. When no one showed up immediately to mop it up, Rizzotti went over and sat on the spot and dried it with her shorts. She had absolutely no time to wait for someone to come and dry the floor. The reaction demonstrated Rizzotti's intensity, but did it mean she would be impatient with her teammates?

In recruiting, Dailey employs the same standard techniques used by her counterpart, Dickenman. She tracks recruits, develops relationships with coaches, watches players perform, sends mail, maintains phone contact, tries to get Geno into the home. One major difference from the UConn men, however, is that the women tend to rely heavily on team members to evaluate and attract a recruit during her campus visit.

"Sometimes when kids go on recruiting visits, they stay in hotels," Dailey says. "Our recruits stay with our players in their rooms, and they spend the majority of their time with the players. Obviously, they meet a lot of people when they are here, but the biggest part of our recruiting is having them spend time with our players.

"Players give us immediate feedback. Our kids have generally never seen the recruit play. We decide who comes on campus based on what our needs are, while our kids base their feeling on what kind of person she is and how she fits into the group."

Pattyson says that when she was a player and a recruit was visiting, she felt it was her personal responsibility to make the player want to come to Connecticut. "It's important to get along with your teammates," Pattyson says. "The other players are like your sisters. You play, travel, run, sweat, do everything together. I always felt it was the coach's job to get the kid to visit and our job was to get the kid to come here. When we had recruits in, my weekend revolved around that recruit. We went out and did things, but it was predicated on what the kid wanted to do. If the kid was fun and crazy, then we could do that. If the kid wanted to sit in and watch movies, we could do that too."

Dailey says she will fill players in about a recruit but does not try to orchestrate the visit. "We just kind of let it happen," she says. "That's the most natural way. The best recruiting weekends are when you feel there isn't a recruit on campus. When Nykesha Sales visited, I didn't feel there was any pressure. She just fit right in like she was already part of the group."

Auriemma's recruiting philosophy and presentation are also founded in individual and group dynamics. In the early days, he played the interpersonal off against what he didn't have, facilities. In later years, he emphasized it over what he did have, success.

"If a kid can choose from any of the absolute five best schools in the country, can go anywhere they want, what is going to make them choose you?" Auriemma asks. "Well, you better have a lot going for you if you want to get that kid. But suppose you don't. What happens if you don't have a nice building? What happens if your library is wrapped in plastic? What happens if you don't have a nice setting like North Carolina? How do you overcome the things you don't have? You stress the people that are here. I want you to come because you want to play for me and you want to be around the people I have assembled. You can go anywhere and be an All-

American. But you will value the people here more than the people you will meet somewhere else.

"When we were recruiting the kids we won the Big East championship with for the first time, well, the roof was leaking in the Field House and we didn't even have our own locker room. So how did we get Kerry Bascom and Laura Lishness and all those kids that helped us go twenty-four and six? They wanted to play for me, and they wanted to play for Chris Dailey, and they wanted to be around the kids we had assembled.

"That attitude hasn't changed. What has changed is that now we can get into the homes of better players. We still give them the same message. You want to go to Virginia, why? Well, they went to the Final Four, so did we. Well, they have a nice building, so do we. They have a great support system, so do we. So now what does it come down to? Well, their academic reputation is a little better than yours. Well, what the hell can I do about that?

"So now you say, well, Rebecca Lobo was tops in her class. Pam Webber was number one in her class. They could have gone to school anywhere in America. Why would their parents let them come here if this wasn't a good school? So if it's more important for you to go to a school because they have a good reputation, that's fine. Then you need to go there. But here's why those kids came here. And if that fits you, then we would love to have you. If not, well, I don't care how good you are, we aren't going to lose any sleep over you. That is the mentality that has brought us the kids we have."

Another major difference between the UConn men and women in recruiting involves numbers. While the men may start out with varying degrees of interest in as many as two hundred players, the women have a much more limited scope.

"We don't recruit in large numbers," Dailey says. "Even when we were bad, we didn't. We hone in on a smaller number and then work really hard, make it almost hard for the kid to say no. We don't have a lot of kids visit that don't end up coming to Connecticut. For instance, last year [1994] we had five kids visit early and we signed four of them. We've taken big chances. We're not the kind of team that has ten backups. The year we recruited Rebecca we were going to either have a great recruiting year or a doo-doo one. There were a couple of other kids we tried to recruit that year who ended up not coming, but we spent the most time with Rebecca and Pam Webber and it paid off. I would have been shocked if Rebecca didn't come here, but you also have those moments right before the signing when you think, if she doesn't come here what are we going to do?"

Eliteness has also broadened the geographical base. "Generally, I don't think women go as far away to school unless there are special circumstances," Dailey says. "Now that we have had success, I can't tell you how many calls we get from kids in Georgia, California. Today, we go after the best. Now if a kid is the best and fits our program, we will go anywhere to get her."

One point on which Dailey and Dickenman agree is that success and national recognition has not diminished the workload or the pressure.

"We may be able to recruit the top players," Dailey says, "only now the competition is Tennessee, Virginia, the top five programs in the country. Once you get to this level, there becomes a smaller pool of kids who can help you. When we were bad, there was a larger number of kids who could help us. The better you get, the smaller the number of kids that can help you and the greater the competition for those kids.

"I don't want to slip. Schools like Virginia or Stanford can replenish just because of the name of the school. We still feel we have to outwork people to get kids. The minute you think you are something, you slip a couple of notches. The minute you overlook the little things, the minute you don't do the things that got you to where you are, then you are missing the boat on what made you successful."

"The tough part is getting the program where it is now," Dickenman says. "The tougher part is maintaining it. If you take a year off mentally or physically from recruiting, don't work as hard, then you are not going to have as good a team down the line. That's why it is so competitive. You want to stay where you are."

17

UConn 2000

To look at the men's and women's basketball programs at the University of Connecticut in 1995 is to feel that a century, not just a decade, has passed since the two teams were perennial losers, since there were rows of empty seats in the stands, since the Field House floor was a garden of rain-soaked towels, since the task force report was written, since Geno Auriemma and Jim Calhoun arrived.

Today, the programs are models off the court as well as on. Success has been maximized in all areas, benefiting not only basketball but the athletic department and the university as a whole. When Calhoun was running his head into the institutional bureaucracy during the early years, he argued time and again that if the basketball team were successful, everyone would benefit. He has been proven correct.

There is no greater evidence of this than a piece of legislation called "UConn 2000," which was passed during the 1995 session of the state legislature. The $1 billion law gives the University of Connecticut the power to issue its own bonds and to spend $980 million over the next ten years on renovations and new construction at its main campus and branches.

While the allocation was long overdue for the state's long-neglected flagship university, it was not coincidental that the problem was finally addressed at a time when the school's basketball teams had achieved national prominence. In pushing for passage of the bill, UConn officials did not hide the fact that they hoped the air of good feeling about the university's basketball teams would translate itself into support. A *Hartford Courant* story on the mobilization effort behind UConn 2000 stated that those involved "had put as much energy into the lobbying effort for the plan as Jennifer Rizzotti expends on a fastbreak."

Reading that newspaper account, Chris Dailey had been taken aback: "Until then it hadn't dawned on me that we had had a political impact," Dailey says. "I thought, wow, when did this happen? Maybe I won't fully comprehend the impact we have had for a long time, but it is bigger than I ever dreamed."

Immediately following a press conference at the state capitol to announce that agreement had been reached on UConn 2000, lawmakers adjourned to the state house chambers to greet the previously invited men's and women's teams. The reception they provided was boisterous, the lawmakers, their staff, and their families pressing the players for handshakes and autographs. Lobo was so besieged she needed a police escort to get through the crowd and back to Storrs for a class.

As Calhoun surveyed the wild scene, his thoughts drifted back to the early days when he was among those pleading with the state for $23 million to build Gampel Pavilion. He also thought about the ifs: "If Cliff Robinson had transferred, if Donyell Marshall hadn't come, if Ray Allen wasn't so special, if Rebecca had made another choice," Calhoun wondered, "where would UConn 2000 be?"

Conversely, Auriemma wondered where UConn basketball would be in the future without UConn 2000.

"We couldn't continue to compete at this level unless something like UConn 2000 occurred," Auriemma says. "Kids aren't coming to the University of Gampel. If they were, we could get any kid in America. The problem is they don't live in Gampel, they don't eat there, they don't go to class in there. So the rest of the university has to be as good as Gampel Pavilion. Here's the analogy I use: Virginia has a pretty good basketball program, right? They can never be better than their school. Same thing for Stanford, Duke, North Carolina. At the places that are really good, basketball is just another good program in the school. Anytime a program becomes better than the university, then you have a problem. And it's a problem that is going to catch up to you and hurt you.

"If I can't go into Rebecca Lobo's house and sell her on the value of this university as a great environment, great education, great faculty, then we are not everything we could be relative to whom we are playing against. If you just want to beat Maine, New Hampshire, fine, don't change. But if you want us to beat the great institutions, then you better be as good as them as an institution. Don't ask us to be better than you are. It's not fair. If you want me to win another National Championship over the next ten years, then I need the resources to recruit another Rebecca Lobo. If I don't have them, then it's not my fault."

If he could choose his legacy at this point in his tenure, Calhoun says it would not be the wins and losses. It would be his part in bringing UConn 2000 to fruition. If athletics is the front porch of the university, as Calhoun once stated, then Connecticut now sees the university as the entryway. "The university is how the whole nation sees our state," Calhoun says. "They see us through the eyes of Rebecca, and Ray Allen's smile, and Donny Marshall being so articulate, and the cuteness of Pam Webber. And what a wonderful, wonderful way that is for people to see Connecticut."

Although the legislators who voted for UConn 2000 were spending a huge chunk of the taxpayers' money, support was widespread. That is because the legislators' regard for the university reflects that of the state population in general. Evidence of the teams' popularity can be seen daily in the ubiquitous UConn T-shirts, UConn hats, UConn bumper stickers, and in the legion of preteen girls wearing UConn game jerseys with Lobo's number 50 on the back. There are also some hard numbers demonstrating how loyalty to UConn's basketball teams extends to the university as well.

A telephone poll done by the University of Connecticut Laboratory for Leisure, Tourism and Sports in the spring of 1995 revealed that two thirds of the state's population, a total of about 1.59 million people, said they follow UConn men's and women's basketball. And 85 percent of those contacted felt basketball had improved the university's overall image. The survey also showed that 91 percent of those contacted saw the university's academic reputation as being good or excellent, and 10 percent said they would be more willing to make a contribution to the university because of the success of the basketball teams. Finally, more than 21 percent of those surveyed—the equivalent of 565,000 adults—said they became interested in applying for admission to UConn because of the basketball teams' success.

During the first half of the 1990s, in-state applications at UConn averaged in the range of 10,491 annually, down somewhat from the 12,752 that were received for the class following the Dream Season in 1989–90. Because of the women's success in 1994–95, another jump is anticipated. The national publicity has also attracted more out-of-state students. Of the 1,897 students in the 1994 freshman class, 24 percent were from out of state, the highest total ever.

Television ratings are yet another indication of the scope of the teams' popularity. In excess of 200,000 television households throughout Connecticut tuned in to the average UConn men's regular-season game during the 1994–95 season. The rating exceeded that for all other types of sports programming and all but the very top prime-time shows. The UConn women averaged more than eighty thousand television households for their regular-season games during that same period, a figure that almost tripled for their NCAA Tournament games.

Success on the court, combined with a modern marketing approach, has also translated into money in the bank:

For the 1986–87 season, Calhoun's first, the UConn Athletic Department budget was $5 million and men's basketball generated $1.05 million in revenue.

Average attendance at nine Hartford Civic Center games was 9,819, more than 6,000 below capacity, the unsold seats representing an annual loss of $300,000.

Television revenue from the Big East Conference was $478,000, while the local television package with Channel 20 paid $50,000 per season.

Income derived from the sale of novelty items such as T-shirts and hats totaled $12,000, and no money was earned from the sale of merchandise featuring the school logo.

The total raised through fund-raising was $500,000.

As for the women, in 1990–91, during the first season admission was charged for their games, revenue from ticket sales brought in $160,957, and expenses totaled $461,424. And that was the year they went to the Final Four for the first time.

The figures for the 1994–95 season are staggering in comparison:

For the 1994–95 fiscal year, the UConn Athletic Department total budget was $12.1 million and men's basketball generated almost $6.1 million in revenue. Included in the men's gross were more than $3.3 million in ticket sales, $1 million from local television and radio contracts, almost $1.6 million from a share of Big East profits, and $137,071 from concession sales and novelties.

The UConn women generated just under $900,000 in total revenue, including $664,793 from ticket sales, $61,000 from local radio and television agreements, and $25,000 from CBS.

Although the figures cannot be credited to any one sport, the men's and women's teams were also mostly responsible for record years in three other areas: fund-raising ($3.7 million), contributions of athletic corporate partners ($1.5 million), and money from licensing and merchandising ($300,000).

Those who play in the men's and women's programs today are reaping the rewards of success.

The practice facilities, the medical treatment, the training and nutrition programs, and the equipment are all first-rate. Each team has its own modern locker room, complete with an adjacent lounge featuring a big-screen television.

More often than not, when the team travels, it does so by charter jet, which is not only less of a hassle but also allows players to return immediately after games so they miss less class time. This is a long way from the days when Calhoun had to fight for a bathroom in the back of the bus.

The academic support system is also light-years away from a system that once basically assumed the majority of players would fail. Today, each team has its own academic adviser to assist student athletes. The advisers travel with the team, conducting mandatory study halls, keeping track of progress, helping with time management, and serving as liaisons with faculty. In addition, advisers coordinate with individual tutors, who also accompany the team to away games if necessary. When the men were on the West Coast for two weeks during the NCAA Tournament, two tutors were flown out to join the team and work with players who were unable to attend class.

When not on the road, the teams have mandatory study halls monitored by the advisers. The sessions are held in the respective teams' individual study halls in Gampel Pavilion, rooms that feature computers.

It seems so long ago that Jim Calhoun had to crack a textbook and personally tutor Cliff Robinson.

Huskymania II

To develop an elite program in the era of big-time, big-stakes college basketball is an extremely difficult undertaking. There are 302 schools that play at the Division I level in this country, and all strive to be successful. All would like to experience the rewards that go along with winning at the highest level: the prestige, the national recognition, the financial windfall. But year in, year out, it seems the same schools occupy the high ground, routinely dismissing those with the impertinence to challenge their domain. Why is that? Why do some institutions win all the time and others not? What do winning programs have that others don't?

Tradition? An important factor to be sure, but no program had more of a winning tradition than UCLA during the 1960s–70s, when the Bruins won ten National Championships in twelve seasons. Why did it take them more than twenty years to win another?

Support? An important factor to be sure, but many schools that provide exemplary services for their athletes are not in the upper echelon.

Facilities? An important factor to be sure, but if a nice building were all it took, why don't all of the edifice-endowed institutions reign?

Reputation? An important factor to be sure, but is there a college in this country held in higher regard than, say, Notre Dame? And when was the last time a Fighting Irish five frightened anyone?

Which brings up another point. Why is it that schools such as Notre Dame or Nebraska are able to excel in football, a much more complex and difficult program to build and maintain, but can't get it done when the ball is round?

The other side of the coin is equally perplexing. Why was the University of Connecticut, which ten years ago did not have much in the way of tradition, support systems, facilities, or reputation, able to become a national power in both men's *and* women's basketball?

"Building a program takes an understanding of what you are looking for," Chris Dailey says. "At the very beginning it is important to bring in very, very solid kids. Kids that are going to go to school and work hard. They may not be the best athletes, but they have a good understanding of dedication and commitment and loyalty to what you are about, what you are trying to do.

"Your first recruiting class is real key in that respect. As you build, you build around them. We started with kids who were maybe not on the Top Twenty recruiting lists. Then, the better we got, the better the player we were able to recruit, provided they fit into what we were doing. Some people get crazy and tend to forget what they are about. They start bringing in all types of players, all styles of play, people who don't fit them, don't fit their personality. So one year they win twenty games, the next they win eight.

"We have been successful because we have remained grounded. It doesn't mean we were not able to make adjustments. We won the National Championship differently than the year we went to the Final Four. We were able to make adjustments in terms of our strengths and weaknesses, but the basics were the same. If you ask anyone, they will tell you our team plays hard. Even when we were bad, we played hard. That has always been our trademark. The difference now is we are playing hard with better players."

The men's program employed a similar philosophy: "We started with a defined plan," Calhoun says. "We had good kids when we came here who kind of got us going the first year. But the biggest thing was that we knew where we wanted to go and we had a pretty good idea how to get there. That's where things like our recruiting theory came in. Another thing was context. The worst thing you can do is try and be somebody else. We were going to do it our way. So I guess the keys would be have a plan, stay the course, get good kids, and don't take any shortcuts along the way."

Again, this sounds easy enough. But then why doesn't every program that uses this approach succeed? Why haven't other schools who have recruited good kids, and worked hard, and been true to themselves not been as successful as

UConn? The answer is that the key is not in the physical plant, or good planning, or purity of purpose, or positive psychology. It's personal and personnel.

What makes a program prosper, or not, is the person at the top, the single-minded individual who has the drive and focus along with the leadership and communication skills to wrestle reality from vision. Why is Nebraska a football power? Tom Osborne. Why didn't UCLA win all those years? No John Wooden. Why did UConn become a basketball power? Jim Calhoun and Geno Auriemma.

If football coaches are really frustrated Napoleons and baseball managers are the blue-collar foremen of the sports world, then basketball coaches are its used-car salesmen. They are sharp, slicked-back, and smooth. Sure, they can bark at players and bait referees, but, more often than not, their preferred method of discourse is the old schmooze. The basketball coach of the nineties must be able to communicate with players, administrators, faculty, fans, parents, media, alumni. He or she must be able to get everybody on board and pulling in the same direction. Personality-wise, these hardwood helmsmen may run the gamut from Captain Ahab to Captain Kangaroo, from Bobby Knight to Dean Smith, but they all have the ability to build consensus.

What is particularly interesting in the case of Calhoun and Auriemma, two men who seem very different on the surface, is the similarity of their backgrounds.

Both came from blue-collar situations and had heavy responsibility thrust upon them at an early age. Calhoun's father died when he was fifteen, leaving him as the male head of the household. Auriemma came to this country when he was seven and quickly had to become his family's outside link to a new culture.

Both men had to elevate themselves, which they did through hard work, Calhoun cutting gravestones, Auriemma working in the steel mills.

Both men established programs based on a trademark work ethic. Both men are extremely demanding of their players, never seemingly satisfied. Both men are driven, Calhoun by the belief in effort and more effort, Auriemma by the siren call of perfection.

Both men have a firm grasp of self and have never forgotten their roots or what got them to where they now are.

Certainly Calhoun and Auriemma deserve, and receive, the lion's share of credit for the rise of UConn basketball. But to review this success story is to be struck by a glaring irony. The man who might be most responsible for the program's elevation has never been given his due. It was John Toner, after all, who sought out, courted, and attracted Jim Calhoun. It was the former athletic director who ultimately gave Geno Auriemma a chance. And yet Toner left the university under a perception of incompetence. Where would UConn basketball be today if John Toner were a lesser judge of people?

In retrospect, if the moment had not been ripe for change, if John Casteen had not created the Task Force on Athletics, if the legislature had not finally come up with the funds for Gampel Pavilion, then the rapid rise the programs made would have been much more difficult, regardless of Calhoun and Auriemma.

While timing may be everything, the times are elusive.

"Who knows when the stars will line up correctly again,"

cautions Tim Tolokan, the UConn sports information director. "For people to assume that success is always going to be there is fantasy. You should cherish every game, every moment, every season. You should embrace it and say this is terrific. You should never take what has happened or what is happening for granted."

ABOUT THE AUTHOR

JIM SHEA has been a writer at *The Hartford Courant* for the past thirteen years. Prior to that he worked as a freelance writer and as a government reporter and political columnist for *The Bristol Press*. Born and raised in Waterbury, Connecticut, he now lives in Harwinton, Connecticut, with his wife, Jan, their two daughters, Lisa and Kaitie, and an untrainable dog that doesn't answer to the name Jake. This is his first book.